The Onyx Boys Adventures

ROCK – PAPER – SCISSORS

Clifford L. Wiggins, Jr.

DEDICATION

*For all my students over the past thirty-six years who
had to listen to my stories - God bless each one of you -
but especially to the Class of 2016 who voted me
"Most Likely to Write a Book"
of all the staff members of Tehachapi High School.
Here it is!*

CONTENTS

PREFACE

Someone once asked just how the writing of these crazy adventures came about. Well, it was two things, really. First, my family and students loved to hear me tell these stories and second, when I got word of Burt's passing it hurt deep inside. We were the best of friends for our time together. I began writing as my way of both coping with his death and remembering him.

I find it amazing that we both ended up working for the school system. Burt became a bus driver, driving the same bus routes we would get kicked off of as kids, while I became an English teacher and coach. Life may have sent us in two different directions but we both never lost our love for hunting, fishing and riding motorcycles.

I will be forever thankful to my friend for helping to shape me into the man I am today. I guess I'm done, as this is getting a bit too sappy. Burt didn't like that sort of stuff – so thanks buddy for all those adventures.

Chapter 1

FULL MOTOCROSS RULES

The town I grew up in - well, I don't know if you could actually call it a town - was very small. Onyx had a year round population of around 15 when we arrived in 1968. In fact, the school bus only picked up one single kid before our family made it a cool half dozen.

Most of the landowners were what you would call "Weekend Warriors." They would come up to stay for a few days or weeks every now and then. They all hired me to water their trees and hula-hoe their weeds. This kept me in soda pop money and snacks at the local store.

I looked forward to summer the most because that's when the Weekend Warriors would ALL come and bring their grandkids. I was always on the lookout for a Best Friend. The only other "kid" in town year-round was already in high school and he was a senior. So, I guess you could say I was the toughest, strongest, fastest and best-looking guy in town - until Burt showed up.

I first met Burt in June of 1968. His family owned a small trailer on the property next to ours. I remember seeing their heavily loaded station wagon pulling up. I was overjoyed to see a boy's Stingray bike tied to the top. Being the friendly type (and wanting to mark my territory quickly) I hopped the fence and strolled over to introduce myself.

"Hi, my name's Cliff and I live next door, what's your name?" I asked.

"My name's Burt," he replied as he tugged on a rope.

"Hey, see that small rocky hill over there?" I said. "I gotta fort on the top and I'll show it to you."

Burt said he'd be glad to go just as soon as he got his stuff unpacked. After helping him unload the car and meeting his folks, we walked back to my trailer to get my bike.

Now, one thing I noticed right away was that Burt's bike was just like mine, only newer. We had both removed those silly chain guards and taken off our mirrors. But one thing struck me as kinda odd. While we were admiring each other's bikes, Burt kept staring at me.

Finally I couldn't take it anymore so I asked, "Whatcha looking at?"

"I was just wondering who's faster: you or me?" was Burt's reply. This was great, finally somebody to race besides my little brother. I wouldn't have to give him a head start! Looking back on it now, the next words out of Burt's mouth should have warned me.

"Full Motocross Rules," he said. "First one to the hill still on his bike wins."

Not wanting to sound like a dumb old country boy, I just replied, "You're on!"

What "Full Motocross Rules" were I hadn't a clue. I guess, looking back, I should of paid more attention to the "still on his bike" part.

Now Rocky Hill sat about a half mile away from the back fence of my property. An old dirt road, actually just two old cow trails stretched side by side over sagebrush and rocks, formed a direct line to Rocky Hill – a little knoll covered with bushes and giant rocks. My little brother, David, and I had built a really cool fort on the very top.

Burt and I agreed to count to three together. On three we hit the pedals and were off. We had gone only a few yards when Burt *bumped* me with his shoulder nearly causing me to meet a large yucca tree face first.

"What in the world are you doing?" I screamed through the dust.

"Full Motocross Rules!" he hollered back.

I immediately retaliated with a right shoulder and the race was on. I only wish video cameras had been invented because this would have made a heck of a film on "What Not to Do." Burt decided to lean right. I decided to lean left. Unfortunately, our handlebars decided to lock together. I remember sagebrush, rocks, blue sky, sagebrush, rocks, blue sky, and then total darkness accompanied by absolute silence. The first thing I saw was Burt's face on the other side of my front wheel. Well, it might have been my front wheel.

"Wow, that was great!" said Burt.

It took us a good five minutes to disengage our bodies and our bikes. A quick check revealed three blown tires, one split lip, several deep scrapes and a cut ear. We looked terrible but we were now fast friends.

"That was a pretty good wreck," I said as we began walking what was left of our bikes back home.

"That was nothing compared to a couple I had last summer," was Burt's reply.

Upon arriving back home, we began the difficult task of putting our bikes back together.

"Hey, Burt," I asked. "Have you ever wanted a motorcycle?"

"I have two at home. I'm bringing them up next weekend," grinned Burt.

"Cool," I smiled as I looked at my new Best Friend.

Chapter 2

BULL TAG

Throughout our time together, Burt and I would often invent some rather innovative "games." Now these games were not the type of activities most kids would play. Bull Tag, without a doubt, was the most dangerous and, in retrospect, the dumbest-most-enjoyable game we ever created.

The idea came one day while we were watching a local rodeo. "If I was a clown I would smack those bulls right on the nose," I said.

Burt leaned over smiled and whispered, "I would smack 'em on the butt and pull their tail."

A few weeks later while hiking home from a fishing trip, we had our opportunity. The path we took to the river crossed through the Smith Ranch and, of course, through their cattle.

Normally, we steered clear of these animals. However, after watching that rodeo, we wanted to see just how close we could get. Since those clowns worked in pairs, we decided to work the same.

We would take turns "distracting" the selected target while the other would sneak in from behind. I was pretty miffed that Burt was the first to touch a cow. It was quite exciting when he slapped that cow's behind and it whirled around on him. Burt must have covered forty yards in less than five seconds. This game soon became too easy.

"I think it's time to go pro," said Burt.

"I think it's time to go for the bulls," he finished as we headed home from the river one afternoon. A quick game of Rock-Paper-

Scissors decided who would go first.

"Just make sure you keep his attention," I said as we began to cross the ranch.

As luck would have it, a stocky little Hereford bull we had nicknamed Blockhead was our intended target for today. We gave him the nickname due to his huge head and short square shaped horns.

The plan was for Burt to approach him from the east. This gave me two advantages. First, the sun would be behind me and thus might impair old Blockhead's vision, and second, the light wind was coming from the east putting me downwind.

The moment old Blockhead saw Burt, he snapped up his head and began to follow Burt's every step. We had agreed that as soon as Burt saw me approaching, he would begin to talk to the bull to drown out any small noise I might make.

"Hey, Blockhead, you're not very smart are you?" Burt began as I made my approach.

Now, I don't know if it was just bad luck, bad timing, or what - maybe bulls have a sixth sense or something. I don't know - but just as my hand was about to make contact with old Blockhead's backside, Burt reached the end of one of his "compliments." Whatever the case, instead of a loud palm smack to the rump, my fingertips barely grazed him as he whirled around to face me.

I immediately put my hand out and shoved Blockhead right in the nose and took off running for the nearest tree. Now, if you have never felt the breath of a bull from inches away, let me tell you - every hair on my body was standing on end. That bull was so close I could feel his snot on my legs and his deep bellow ringing in my ears.

I zigged. I zagged. I dipped and I darted for what seemed like a full five minutes before I literally dove into that tree. I grabbed the first branch I could and swung my body like a trapeze performer, right in to the blur of green above me. The twigs and branches that raked my arms, legs, chest, and face didn't bother me at all. I wrapped myself around that tree as tight as I could.

Heart pounding and chest heaving, I looked down. Old Blockhead was standing right below me. He was pawing the dirt, shaking his head and snorting snot everywhere.

"That was so cool, that was sooo cool!" Burt hollered from his perch in another tree some fifty yards away.

"Where were you?" I hollered back. "How come you didn't help me?"

"What was I supposed to do?" was my friend's reply. I really didn't know what it was I wanted him to do. I was just mad and scared.

In addition to being gifted with speed, we also learned that day that bulls are very patient creatures. Old Blockhead kept pacing back and forth underneath those two trees for the better part of the next two hours, before finally lumbering off.

Burt and I hit the ground at full speed and quickly reached the fence, and safety. After catching our breath we both broke into laughter and high fives as we began our walk home.

"It's your turn next time," I said with an air of triumph.

"But you missed!" was Burt's reply.

Chapter 3

SNAKES!

I hated snakes. I just couldn't stand the sight of them. Burt, on the other hand, loved them. He had four or five of them as pets. He kept them in cages in his garage. He even went as far as to buy a five-foot baby boa constrictor. However, we both agreed that rattlesnakes had to be killed on sight.

Most Saturday mornings during the summer would find me working in our family garden: hoeing weeds, tilling the soil or harvesting a crop. Burt would inevitably pop up on a fence post to let me know where he was going and what he would be doing so I could join him when I finished.

One early July morning he announced from his fence post perch, "I'm going fishing at the river. I'll be at the twin oaks."

I finished my chores, gathered my stuff and set out to meet him about an hour later. During the summer, Burt and I were somewhat allergic to clothes. Typical summer fishing attire consisted of a pair of Levi cutoffs. That's it. No shoes, no shirts.

The only other thing we wore was a pillowcase cut in half with a piece of rope looped through holes and tied around our waist. I guess you could call it an early version of a fanny pack. We just called it our fishing bag. We put stringers, hooks, bait, lures, bobbers and the occasional snack in it. Armed with my trusty Zebco 44, I started off.

The river lay about a half a mile from my front gate. Jogging down the path across the highway and rounding the last bend in the trail, I froze dead in my tracks. Not five feet from me in the middle of the trail lay two of the biggest rattlesnakes I'd ever seen. Both were curled up side by side with their heads tucked neatly within the coil.

I was scared to death, afraid to move. I couldn't go forward, nor could I back up. I couldn't do anything. My mind was racing. Then it came to me, I'd whistle. Burt and I had made a pact a long time before to whistle when we needed each other.

As quietly as possible I whistled "Whip-Poor-Will." The snakes remained still. I waited a good ten seconds before letting loose another whistle, just a tad louder this time. Suddenly, to my relief I heard in the distance Burt's reply. I whistled a third time. Thankfully, the snakes hadn't moved.

Burt's head and shoulders appeared, coming up the trail. I waved my arms frantically, placing my fingers to my lips, pointing to the ground and moving my finger in an "S" shape.

"What?" hollered Burt.

"Snakes, rattlesnakes." I whispered as loudly as possible.

Burt came fully into view and quickly approached from the far side. When he saw the snakes, he froze, too.

"Do you have any rocks or sticks by you?" he whispered.

"No, do you?" was my hushed reply.

Burt shook his head no. He slowly walked toward the snakes. When I tried to whisper to him to stop – that what he was doing was insane - he just raised a finger to his lips and continued to inch his way closer to the snakes.

About three feet away, Burt reached into his back pocket and pulled out a strip of cloth. In one fluid motion he tied a headband around his head. Assuming a kung fu, martial-arts-like stance, he began to breathe deeply while moving his arms in a slow, windmill-like fashion.

Bowing his legs he lowered himself to within inches of the snakes. He paused with hands outstretched. Then he mouthed the words, "I'm going to grab them and squeeze their heads off."

This was nuts! Burt took two slow deep breaths and with hands moving like lightning, reached down and snatched up both snakes.

They curled around his arms, thrashing and rattling like crazy.

"Are you plain loco?!" I yelled at him.

Burt screamed at the top of his lungs. With his arms rigid and muscles bulging, he snapped violently in a downward motion and suddenly two snakes, minus their heads, lay on the dirt in front of him.

"They can still bite you!" I screamed, "What the heck are you doing?"

Burt just threw back his head and laughed. He opened his hands wide to show me they were empty. I stood in stunned amazement.

"I killed them both with rocks an hour ago. I cut their heads off and coiled them up in the trail just to scare you! You oughtta seen your face when I grabbed them!"

Chapter 4

SEVEN DUCKS

When it came to duck hunting, Burt and I were completely addicted. We bought every magazine that had anything to do with ducks. We believed ourselves to be the two most ingenious and successful duck hunters in the entire Kern River Valley. Burt and I hunted them on the lake, in the marshes, on private ponds, and at the nearby South Fork of the Kern River.

Now hunting "river ducks" was extremely challenging. In addition to dealing with trees, cows, and the occasionally angry rancher, you also had to figure out how to retrieve your birds from fast-moving water. We tried several methods: ropes, nets, and inner tubes, each with mixed results. However one Thanksgiving, Burt came up with one legendary shot and an even more amazing method of retrieval.

We began our hunt by walking up river to a spot we'd dubbed "Mallard Creek." Mallard Creek was about one and a half to two miles east of Onyx. It got its name in honor of my first duck ever.

Our plan was to walk together along the south bank. We had tried hunting on opposite sides before. Two problems ended that approach. First we often argued over who shot which duck and second it proved…well…dangerous. It's hard to hunt when you're laying face down on the ground.

We jumped a pair of ducks early and each somehow managed to shoot the opposite bird. A few yards further down river I managed to drop a beautiful Canvasback when he exploded nearly under my feet.

The next half hour produced nothing but a heavy drizzle. Being up one bird I was feeling pretty sorry for my friend.

"I'll tell you what, Burt, I..."

Burt cut me off in mid sentence with a sharp, "Shut up and listen."

In the distance I heard what made him so excited. It sounded like a room full of women laughing. Burt and I made our way slowly and quietly to a small knoll and crawled on our bellies to the top.

What we saw made our hearts flutter. Floating tightly together against the far bank was a flock of over twenty Mallards. Burt and I slid on our butts back down the knoll.

"What do you wanna do?" I asked my friend.

"We crawl back to the top and on three we shoot." was Burt's reply.

Looking back I guess I should have got some clarification as to Burt's idea of three. We reached the top and lying on our backs we looked at each other and nodded. One, two, th...BLAM!

I jumped to my feet and got off my first shot as Burt was firing his second. Ducks were flying everywhere. My first dropped a bird neatly on the bank, my second missed, but my third dropped a beautiful male, almost straight above me. The bird landed only a few feet away.

"What the heck Burt, what happened to three?" I yelled through the rain and gunpowder.

Burt was busy taking off his shoes and socks and quickly replied, "I said shoot on three, not count to three and then shoot."

Anger had been replaced by confusion. "What are you doing?" I asked as Burt now stood before me buck-naked.

"I'm not losing any of my birds!" Burt stated as he pointed to the river.

"Come on, get your clothes off and help me," he yelled over his shoulder as he slid down the knoll to the river. I couldn't reply as I was stunned by what I saw. Lying on the river floating in a little eddy were seven ducks.

"I can't believe you got seven," I managed to say as the cold water swirled around my friend's head.

14

"You shot 'em, you get 'em," I said as I picked up my second bird. I sat down and watched in amazement as Burt emerged from the water with all seven of his birds.

Burt quickly dressed and as we jogged towards my house I said, "Shoot, Burt, who needs a dog?"

Chapter 5

ISLAND BOAT

I'm not really sure which one of us gave birth to this idea, but it was without a doubt one of our finest.

Burt and I were avid duck hunters. We liked hunting while walking the river, but we loved hunting from Burt's little aluminum boat on Lake Isabella.

On the lake we would drop anchor somewhere in the shallows where the South Fork of the Kern entered into the lake, cover ourselves with our homemade camouflage tarp (an old gray tarp with black patches spray painted on), and wait for some birds to fly over.

One morning out on the lake Burt said, "We need to see them coming from all directions like from a blind."

I recollect that somewhere in the conversation the term "floating island" was used. Poof, we had our plan.

"We can build the framework out of 1 by 2's, then staple reeds and brush to it, and make a little open spot at both ends for each of us to shoot from."

It took us the better part of a week to build our "island." We drilled and bolted 18 1x2's vertically around the boat. Burt had me stand in the boat with my shotgun and turn a full circle to measure for the correct height. Since Burt and I were the same height we settled on about 35 inches. That would put the top of our island at chest high.

Our next set of 1 by 2's we placed horizontally around the top of our vertical posts. By using twine and bailing wire we were able to bend them into shape. Next we stapled reeds and brush all around.

"Wow, she sure looks good," we both agreed as we admired our creation.

In order to get an early start I ran over to my house, grabbed my hunting vest, shotgun, shells, jacket, and canteen and loaded them in Burt's Rambler.

"Is your trolling motor all charged up?" I asked Burt.

"It's still full from the last time. Meet me here at 4:30am sharp," he said.

Burt was sitting in the Rambler when I walked up the next morning.

"You're three minutes late," was his greeting as he checked his annoying Timex whose gold stretch band always adorned his left wrist.

"I grabbed us some grub," I said holding up a brown paper bag.

"Hey, peanut butter and bananas make a tasty breakfast," smacked Burt between bites.

Onyx is only about seven miles from the lake, so we were there pretty quickly. Burt backed the trailer down to the water's edge and our "island" drifted free.

We parked the Rambler and loaded our gear through a hole we had left along one side. Burt fired up his little outboard motor, while I stood in the front and directed him to our spot.

Once there, we cut the engine, dropped anchor and floated in the silent darkness. We had timed it perfectly. Within minutes, the darkness gave way to light as the sun began to climb over Walker Pass in the east.

We had been sitting there only a few minutes when I saw a flying "V" of about 10 ducks gliding down towards us.

"Burt…" I whispered.

"I got them," he replied.

We positioned ourselves quickly.

"I'll take the lead duck," said Burt.

"I'll take the third one on the right," I countered.

"We go on three, my count," whispered Burt. "One, two, three..." Burt and I fired as one. As the sound echoed off the lake, two birds tumbled from the sky.

"That's the way to start our day," Burt shouted triumphantly.

We retrieved our birds using a fishing net attached to a piece of ten foot PVC pipe (an earlier invention) and fired up the outboard to cross over to a wide spot where the river met the lake. We had traveled maybe a hundred yards when the engine coughed, sputtered then went silent.

"Uh, Cliff. We got a problem," came Burt's rather frustrated voice. "We ran out of gas."

"Where's your spare gas can, just fill 'er up," I said.

"That's the problem. I forgot it back at the Rambler," confessed Burt.

"That's ok. We can use the electric trolling motor."

"No we can't. It's dead, too, " stated Burt sheepishly.

"I thought you said it was fully charged!" I fired back just a tad frustrated myself now.

"Well, I was wrong!" shot back my friend.

Always a thinker, I said, "Okay, break out the paddles."

"They are in the Rambler as well," said Burt dejectedly.

"Looks like we're swimming her back," I stated as I began to untie my shoes. We stripped down to our underwear in the cold November air. Both of us tumbled out of the boat and instantly regretted it.

"Geez Louise, this is cold," I shouted from my side of the boat. Burt and I grabbed onto our "island" and began to swim for shore. Thank goodness it was only a couple hundred yards until we could stand and walk her onto the beach. Both of us wasted no time putting our clothes back on.

"I'll go get the Rambler. You stay with the boat," Burt hollered over his shoulder as he began to jog away. He hadn't gone 50 feet when he began to pat his pockets.

"I can't find my keys," shouted Burt. We searched the boat for a good half hour...nothing.

"Did you check your vest?" I asked hopefully. Burt quickly grabbed his vest and found them in the second pocket he checked.

"Okay, now I will be back with the Rambler," said Burt as he headed for his car.

I was just waiting for Burt, when I noticed a flock of birds heading right for me. I slowly rose up and watched for them to come into range. I zeroed in on the lead bird and fired, quickly pumped in another round and fired again. Two for two: a mallard drake and a hen. Both fell over land and I quickly recovered them.

Moments later, Burt pulled up in the Rambler, hopped out and asked, "Was that you shooting?"

"Sure was buddy, two for two," I said proudly.

Well, old Burt was just a bit upset. "Next time you go get the Rambler and I'll stay with the boat."

I replied, "Maybe next time you shouldn't forget the gas."

Chapter 6

ASK AND YE SHALL RECEIVE
(PRINCE'S POND #1)

I've often heard fisherman talk about their Honey Hole: a place on a river or along the shore of a lake that never fails to yield fish, lots of fish. Hunters also have their secret spots that always produce results. When it came to duck hunting nothing came close to Prince's Pond.

The Prince Ranch was located where the south fork of the Kern River emptied into Lake Isabella. A thick forest of cottonwood trees hid their pond. Burt and I grew up hearing of this magical duck heaven.

We also grew up with the knowledge that no one was allowed on the property. We'd heard stories of how people had been caught after firing their first shot. We had driven by the ranch and stopped to try and figure out how to park along the highway, hike the mile or so to the pond, hunt, and then some how evade capture.

One November day, Burt and I were duck hunting on Lake Isabella in our Island Boat. As was our custom, we had stuffed it full of sagebrush, tree branches, and covered ourselves and the bottom of the boat in leaves.

The morning had produced a total of six ducks. I had shot 4 mallards (three drakes and a hen) while Burt had dropped a pair of male canvasbacks. The morning had also provided one dead battery on our electric trolling motor.

As we slowly paddled our floating island back to shore, singing the Gilligan's Island theme song, we watched several nice flocks of ducks and one batch of Canadian Honkers hover and land on Prince's Pond.

"We gotta find a way to get to that pond," lamented Burt.

"I don't wanna get arrested. My dad would whip my butt and take away my gun, plus we'd have to pay a fine and we'd lose our licenses," I retorted back.

"There's just gotta be a way," said Burt emphatically.

"Look," I said, "even if we somehow did manage to get on the pond, how are we gonna retrieve our ducks, and get all the way back to the car without getting caught?"

I could see Burt's mind working to come up with an answer. His eyebrows would rise up and his face would brighten up for a moment but eventually the eyebrows would fall and the corners of his mouth would settle back into a deep, brooding countenance.

After watching several of these facial cycles I finally said, "Hey, why don't we just go ask real polite-like for permission? Remember when we asked Mrs. Smith?" Gwynn Smith owned some of the best quail hunting land around Onyx and had given us permission to hunt on her property.

"Come on, Burt. It worked before. It might work again. Just let me do all the talking."

Once we put our "floating island" on its trailer, we headed straight to the Prince Ranch to carry out our plan.

"I hope Mr. Prince isn't as mean and big as everybody says he is," stated Burt as we walked up to the front porch.

I was full of confidence as I knocked on the front door but that feeling quickly faded as three gigantic dogs came barreling and snarling around the corner of the house, making a beeline straight for us. As we turned to face our imminent and certain demise, we were suddenly startled by a deep, booming voice behind us.

"Duke, Lady, Gus, sit!" We stared in wonderment as those three beasts sat immediately down without a whimper.

"What on earth is that contraption sitting on your trailer?" the voice continued. Burt and I turned around and saw this mountain of a man, hands on hips staring at us.

"Aaa... That's our duck hunting boat," I managed to mumble.

"Does she work?"

"It works great...well as long as we don't run out of gas and our trolling motor stays charged," I said staring pointedly at Burt.

"What can I do for you boys?"

Gathering all the courage I could muster, I just came straight to the point, "We would like permission to hunt on your pond, sir."

Now, if you have ever had to stand in front of the principal or a highway patrol officer, you know the feeling. Your mouth feels like cotton - dry as sand - yet your body is sweating buckets. He just stared at us; first at me, then at Burt, then at me again, then at Burt for what seemed like forever.

Finally, he broke into a big old grin, tilted his hat back and said, "You're the first people to ever have the decency to come to the house and ask."

The next words out of his mouth were just magical. "Sure, you boys can hunt the pond but there are a few rules. First, you gotta park outside the gate. Second, I can't let you use your boat but there's a little rowboat at the dock I use that you can retrieve your birds with. And finally, I do not want you shooting before sunup. One last thing, I am only giving you two permission. Wait, what are your names anyway?"

"My name is Cliff and this is Burt," I answered.

"Now, both of you can swim, right? I don't want you on or near that pond if you can't."

We both solemnly nodded and said we could. Then I added, "We would like to hunt tomorrow if that's okay."

He let us know that would be fine and we shook hands and thanked him once again. Burt and I climbed into the Rambler and headed for home.

"Prince's Pond. We get to hunt Prince's pond," was all Burt said the whole way home.

Chapter 7

THE BEST HUNTING TRIP EVER
(PRINCE'S POND #2)

Burt and I were like kids on Christmas morning. You know the feeling. Now that we had permission from Mr. Prince, all we could think about was getting to the pond and getting out on that water. This was going to be our best hunting trip ever! Well, that's what we thought.

That night, after we had cleaned our birds, we drew up a plan of attack for the next day's hunt. We decided, or should I say old Burt insisted that we leave at 4am. He figgered that would put us at the pond by 4:30am and we would be there when the sun rose at 5am.

"Why? We don't need to be that early," I protested.

"No, it's perfect," he countered, "We can hike in by flashlight, find the best spot, and hide under the camo tarp. That way when it's light enough, we can ease out from under the tarp and start shooting."

It was hard to find fault with Burt's logic, so we said good night and agreed tomorrow was gonna be one of our best hunting days ever.

"See ya at four," I hollered as I headed for my house.

I arrived at Burt's at 3:45am only to see his outline sitting in the front seat of the Rambler. Perhaps I should have checked if he was awake before I tossed my backpack and canteen into the bed of the truck. Burt shot out of the front seat with a load roar.

Our drive to the lake was rather quiet, punctuated with my, "I'm sorry," and "No, I didn't do that on purpose."

The hike in was an adventure. Burt's flashlight blinked out before we had gone 50 yards and we had to feel our way along the shore. What should have taken around 10 minutes took us almost a half hour.

I was glad it was dark so Burt couldn't see the faces I was making behind his back every time he said, "Sorry about the flashlight." We were both glad to finally get under the tarp.

"Just think, in less than an hour, ducks are gonna be all around us. This is gonna be great." said Burt excitedly.

"Hope we don't fall asleep," was my simple reply.

Funny thing about dreams, they just seem to come whenever they want to come. The crowd was chanting, "Wiggy, Wiggy, Wiggy!" as I was scoring my fourth touchdown; a beautiful zigging and zagging 80 yard run when Burt's elbow to my ribs woke me.

"Time to hunt. Sun's coming up," he whispered.

We both slowly slid the tarp to the side and gradually rose to our knees in the marsh reeds. Floating in a tight bunch no more than ten yards away was a flock of mallard ducks.

"On three," I whispered. "One, two, three."

Burt and I fired 3 shots each as fast as we could. True duck hunters say it's not sporting to shoot birds not in flight, but we never felt that way. We liked to take home as many as we could bag. Roasted duck was one of Burt's mom's specialties. We counted five birds floating on the pond.

"Too bad you missed one," Burt stated.

"I didn't miss. You did! " I answered sharply. We settled our dispute the usual way with a quick round of Rock-Paper-Scissors.

"Three for me and two for you, buddy. Let's go find that boat," I said with a smug smile.

As Burt mumbled something I didn't quite catch, it suddenly dawned on me (us) that it was snowing. In fact, the ground was already lightly covered.

"Good thing we got a boat. I wouldn't want to have to swim in this weather," said Burt as we untied Mr. Prince's little rowboat. We both thought it wise to leave our gear under the tarp.

"I'm taking my gun, just in case," Burt said as I placed mine under the tarp.

With Burt up front directing, and me rowing, we soon had four of the five birds in the boat. Our fifth and final bird had floated about three to four feet into the marsh reeds. I rowed us as close as I could, but that still left us about four feet short.

"If I stand on the tip of the boat and use an oar, I can reach it," said Burt with confidence.

I was about to tell him to wait so I could move to the opposite corner of the boat to counter balance, but before I could get the words out of my mouth, Burt hopped onto the tip of the boat.

His loud "Noooo!" was cut off as the boat flipped and the ice cold water swallowed my head. By the time I came up and grabbed ahold of our upside down boat, turned, and spit out the water I'd swallowed, I found Burt had already rescued all five of our birds. His blue face peered over the other side.

"Let's get this thing turned over and get to the car," I said through chattering teeth.

"I gotta get my gun first. I got it between my feet," said Burt. He ducked under water and popped right back up holding his gun. We flipped the boat over, threw our birds in and climbed in.

Once back at shore we made straight for the Rambler, jumped in and fired up the heater. We both stripped down to our underwear and tried to ring all the water we could out of our clothes. Twenty minutes with the heater cranked to full blast brought the feeling back to our fingers and toes.

"Let's go home and get some dry clothes and come back later for our stuff," I suggested.

Burt was in total agreement. We headed home, thankful that our ordeal was almost over. Then the old Rambler coughed and coasted silently to the side of the road as Burt groaned, "This isn't happening!"

"How can you be out of gas? You are always running out of gas!" I wailed.

Neither one of us wanted to put our wet clothes back on and step out into the snow but jogging in the snow in our underwear was not an option. So we climbed out of the nice warm car and began the journey home. Thankfully, we had run out of gas barely a half mile away.

"Well, we need to add Rambler gas to our pre-hunt check list, along with a charged battery, and two fully charged flashlights," I said as we plodded along.

"Yep, and maybe an extra set of clothes," answered Burt.

Thus ended "The Best Hunting Trip Ever."

Chapter 8

FLOAT TUBES
(PRINCE'S POND #3)

Our first season hunting on Prince's Pond had taught Burt and I two really important lessons: first, it pays to respect others by asking permission to hunt on their property and second, little aluminum boats flip over really easily. Well, I guess we learned three things – always come prepared with extra gas, dry clothes, and spare keys.

The new hunting season was only a week away so Burt and I decided to drop by the Prince's ranch to make sure we still had permission to hunt. As we pulled up, we saw Mr. Prince splitting wood next to the house.

"Hi, Mr. Prince. We just wanted to make sure we could still hunt the pond this year, " I said as we walked up and shook hands.

"Good to see you boys. Sure, you can hunt the pond again this season. Just keep being careful and you can hunt as much as you want," he replied with a smile. We thanked him again and climbed back in the Rambler.

"Let's go take a look at the pond and see how she looks this year," Burt said as we pulled away.

"Boy, I bet old Mr. Prince wouldn't call us careful if he knew all the stuff that happened last season," I said sheepishly.

We parked the Rambler by the gate and hiked in to see the pond. The first thing we noticed was how much more water there was than last year. The second thing we noticed was the aforementioned little aluminum boat was nowhere to be seen.

'Hey, where's the boat?" I asked as my eyes scanned the pond. We decided to split up and search. Burt headed west and I headed around the eastern shore.

I was nearly half way around the pond when I heard Burt holler, "Found it!"

I jogged around to where he stood pointing out into some heavy reeds some fifty yards from shore.

"It must have drifted free during the winter and got stuck out there. What are we gonna do now?" I said with frustration.

"No, this is perfect. We can try out an idea I've had since last season. We are going to make us some Float Tubes," Burt smiled.

"Those things are pretty expensive and I don't have that kind of cash. My dad already said I have to pay for my own shells this year," I complained.

"Just don't you worry. I've got this all figured out. We can get a couple of inner tubes and use some rope, trash bags and duct tape and make our own," Burt stated as we walked back.

I had to admit this sounded pretty good to me. Burt would be in his and I would be in mine and I wouldn't have to worry about him flipping me into the pond again.

The next day we picked up all our supplies and headed back to Burt's house to build our Float Tubes. After inflating the tubes we used some rope to build us a seat across the bottom.

"Wait. What are we gonna do for waders for our legs?" I asked. That was a good question. We discussed putting trash bags on our legs but that would take too much time.

"Why don't we just make these into our own little boats," Burt replied. Again this sounded pretty good. We used some more rope to build a web-like bottom for our tubes and followed that with several layers of trash bags and a whole lot of duct tape. We realized we would need some paddles so we covered some old tennis rackets with duct tape.

"Let's take them to the river and practice with them," Burt said excitedly.

Our test run produced several small leaks, which we quickly patched – with more duct tape, of course. It also created a tough choice. We found sitting with our legs stretched out over the front of the tubes gave us better stability but sitting Indian style inside the tube gave us more control.

We loaded up our tubes and drove down to Prince's pond and carried them down, tying them securely to some trees a few yards from the water.

"These puppies will be right here waiting for us tomorrow. This is going to be so cool," I said as we walked back to the Rambler.

We agreed to meet at 5am the next morning. As always, old Burt was sitting in the Rambler when I walked up at 4:50am. Having scared him numerous times before, he had parked facing my house so he could see me coming.

"I had my mom make us some scrambled eggs and bacon sandwiches," said Burt holding up a brown paper bag.

"Sweet, but I am too excited to eat right now. We can save them for later."

"Fine by me. Let's get going," he answered as he fired up the Rambler.

We arrived at the pond and quickly placed our tubes in the water and loaded up our gear. After tossing in a couple of armfuls of leaves for cover, we began to paddle out on to the pond. We agreed to face Lake Isabella to be able to see the birds as they glided to the pond, positioning ourselves just outside the reeds.

"Hey, when we are done hunting we can use our tubes to retrieve Mr. Prince's little boat for him," I whispered.

"Good thinking," said Burt.

In hindsight, I should not have agreed with Burt's next idea.

"Let's tie our tubes together side by side. That will makes us a lot more stable."

Forgetting my earlier enlightenment that it would be wiser if Burt would be in his own tube and I would be in mine, we quickly tied our tubes together and sat there floating in the quiet gray dawn.

"This is awesome," Burt said as the first rays of the sun hit the treetops around us. I had to agree. It really was a beautiful sight to watch the sun bounce off all those big yellow leaves.

My moment communing with nature ended when Burt whispered, "Birds coming in at eleven o'clock."

"I got them, I count 14. I will take the third one on the left," I answered.

"I'll take the second one on the right," Burt replied.

"We go on three, my count," said Burt. "One, two, three!"

Burt and I fired as one. Looking back on it now, we should have practiced SHOOTING from our tubes. We quickly discovered that firing a shotgun while leaning back in a floating inner tube is... well, stupid. The recoil from both our blasts flipped our harnessed tubes over backwards into the icy cold water.

Now if you've never experienced the feeling of being suddenly plunged underwater holding a shotgun while tied to someone else who is also experiencing a high state of panic, let me tell you – it's no fun.

Once I untangled myself and my gun from the tubes and their webbing, I fought my way to the surface all the while trying not to be drowned by Burt who was attempting to free himself too. When I finally managed to get my head above water, I opened my eyes to see the tubes had floated a few feet away. I sloshed over to them, tossed my gun in and grabbed on.

"Burt," I sputtered looking around.

"Over here," he called. I turned to my left to see him struggling towards me with his gun held above him and both of our birds in his other hand. He made it to the tubes and tossed his gun and the birds into the tubes alongside my gun.

"Come on! Let's kick our way to shore and get out of this water," I chattered through my teeth.

"No, the boat is closer. We can get in and then tow our stuff in."

We managed to get the boat out of the reeds, tie our tubes to the stern, and paddled as fast as we could for the shore. Once we hit shallow water, we both jumped out and sloshed everything up on to the shore. Then we sprinted to the Rambler, its cab, and its heater. Having experienced this sorta thing before, we came prepared this time each bringing along an extra set of dry clothes and shoes. We quickly changed and hopped inside to fire up the heater.

"You better not have lost your keys," I said as I wrapped myself in an old blanket Burt had tossed in as well.

"No problemo, buddy. I left them right here under my seat" Burt said as he produced the keys and placed them in the ignition.

"I also have plenty of gas and our lunch is right here, " he said nodding at the brown bag between us.

I sat in shock watching Burt turn the key again and again. Utter silence.

"How? How? How can your battery be dead? How?" I shouted.

"I thought for sure I turned my lights off," was his only reply as we took the long walk to Mr. Prince's house to ask him to jump our battery.

Chapter 9

RIVER FROGS

For two boys who loved to hunt and fish, Onyx just had to be the perfect place to grow up. In the early 1970s we had fantastic quail, chukar, and dove hunting all within a mile of our two front doors. Another plus? The South Fork of the Kern River (a mere half mile jog away), which provided us with ducks and fish. It wasn't long, however, until we discovered another treasure – frogs.

Burt and I were returning home late one summer evening from a very successful trout-fishing trip. We had hiked all the way up the river above Canebrake and fished our way home. I had three nice rainbows on my stringer and Burt had two. Of course, he kept reminding me – it seemed every few minutes – that both of his were much bigger than mine.

We were crossing the river back at Onyx when Burt suddenly shouted and leaped backwards, knocking me flat onto my backside into the river.

"What the heck did you do that for?" I hollered as I picked myself out of the water.

"Sorry, but I thought it was a snake. It just jumped out from under me," he replied.

"What did?" I asked.

"A big, old frog, Come on, let's catch him!" Burt said as he sloshed after our frog. Now, trying to catch a frog in the daylight is hard enough but at dusk, well, it's downright impossible.

"Lets go home, get our flashlights, make us some frog gigs and then come back," suggested Burt.

"Ok. Sounds like fun to me. But what are we gonna do with the frogs we catch?" I asked.

"We're gonna eat them. I hear if you fry them up they taste like chicken," Burt answered.

I wasn't too sure about that but heck, I would try anything… once.

After cleaning our fish and eating dinner we met back at Burt's to construct our frog gigs. We duck-taped about a 6-inch piece of two by two to the end of a couple of old rake handles. Once they were secure we drove five eight-penny nails through the two by two and …Poof! We had us some gigs.

"These actually look pretty good. Let's go practice on some tomatoes in the garden," Burt suggested.

Burt picked a couple tomatoes and we both took turns gigging them. Those nails speared the tomatoes with a satisfying "splooch." The sacrifice of two tomatoes was a small price to pay to find out our homemade gigs worked great.

"That was good thinking to use five nails instead of three, that way we have a better chance of spearing them," I said.

"Yep, those frogs are gonna croak," Burt said with a smile.

We hopped into the Rambler and drove back down to the river.

Finding the frogs turned out to be the easy part. Actually gigging them, well, that took a lil' more time. After about five or six jabs each produced nothing but mud, we decided we might be better off throwing our gigs like spears.

"We can take turns, one can spotlight them and the other can spear them," Burt concluded.

This worked to perfection as we both bagged two frogs each in the next four attempts. It was Burt's turn to gig when I spotted a huge old dude under a cottonwood tree that had fallen over into the river.

"If you climb out on the tree you can be right above him. There is no way you can miss him," I instructed my friend. Old Burt climbed out on that tree without a problem.

"Shine that flashlight right on him. This is like shooting fish in a barrel," Burt said with a grin. Burt raised his gig and let it fly.

"Got him!" Burt shouted as he sprang down from the tree. He held up his gig to reveal a monster frog wriggling away.

"This is the biggest one yet," he boasted.

Unfortunately, that was the moment that old frog wriggled free from the gig and splashed back into the water. Burt wasted no time in thrusting his gig after the errant frog.

Suddenly the quietness of the night was shattered by a toe-curling, hair-raising scream. In Burt's excitement to re-gig his monster frog he had gigged his own foot as well. I made my way to him and aimed the flashlight beam on his right foot. He had impaled the frog with 3 of the nails and his foot with the other two.

"Take hold of the gig and when I tell you to… yank it out," Burt winced. He carefully removed his shoe, then his shirt.

"Why'd you take your shirt off?" I asked rather confused.

"I'm gonna wrap it tight like a tourniquet to stop the bleeding," was his slow, steady reply.

"Okay, on three…one, two, three," whispered Burt.

I yanked the gig free and Burt let out another guttural scream. We wrapped his foot as tight as we could.

"You'll have to drive us back and help me wake up my mom. She ain't gonna be too happy about this," Burt said through clenched teeth.

I tried to support him, but he couldn't put any weight on his foot at all, so I carried him piggyback style and hauled him to the Rambler.

Once home, we woke his mom to explain what happened. After a few rather unladylike comments, she had me put Burt back in the Rambler once again.

"You get home. I'm going to take him to the emergency room," she said.

The next morning I went over to check on my buddy.

"Hey Burt, how'd it go at the hospital?" I asked as I walked up to his garage.

"I got a total of seven stitches and a tetanus shot. No real damage. My mom is still pretty mad but she is excited to try frying those frogs up," Burt said as he was hopping around this huge packing crate.

"What's in the box?" I asked as Burt pried off the lid and began to smile from ear to ear.

"This is my new shotgun shell loader. I'm gonna make us some Super Shells. Those Canadian Geese are not gonna fly away this year."

"Cool. Super Shells, " I said with a grin.

Chapter 10

SUPER SHELLS

The morning after our rather eventful frog gigging adventure, I dropped by to help Burt with his new shotgun shell reloader. We unpacked the crate and set about putting the various parts neatly on his workbench.

"Not only will we save money on shells, we can also make us some Super Shells by adding just a bit more gunpowder. That should give us a better chance of bagging our first Canadian Geese. You read me these instructions and we will have this baby together in no time," he said excitedly.

Four hours and several arguments later we finally had every little spring, lever, nut and bolt in its proper location.

"Grab that milk crate full of empty shells and let's load up a few to try it out," ordered Burt.

"I'm going to make three different kinds of shells: regular ones using the exact amount of powder, extra strong using another eighth grams of powder and some Super Shells using another sixth."

"How are we gonna tell them apart?" I asked.

"That's easy," said Burt. "I'm putting one dot on the regular shells, two on the extra loads, and three on the Super Shells."

This all sounded pretty good but I wasn't one hundred percent sure about how these things would work out.

"Burt, I don't want to try these things in my Dad's gun until I know they are safe and if you damage your gun we can't hunt at all this year," I said rather hesitantly.

"I was thinking the same thing. That's why I'm going to use my Dad's old single shot 12 gauge. He never uses it anymore any way," he replied as we gathered up our hunting gear and his Dad's old gun.

"Here, put these in your vest. We can use these as targets," Burt handed me four tin cans from his trashcan.

As we walked over to Camel Mountain (the mountain just east of Onyx that looks like a two hump camel) I was trying to figure out a way to let Burt have the "honor" of taking the first shot. Truth is, I was just a tad afraid of our new shells. Thankfully, old Burt decided that for us.

"I wanna take the first shot. It's my shell loader, so I should get the first shot," he said as we hit the base of the mountain.

"That's fine by me," I replied with relief.

We placed the tin cans at twenty-foot intervals. We would use the Super Shells on the cans furthest away. Burt loaded a regular, single-dot shell, aimed and fired. The can exploded on impact.

"These work fine. Here, you take a shot," he said as he handed me his Dad's gun. I loaded up a single-dot shell, took aim at the next can and fired. It, too, exploded on impact.

"Well, it's time to try the double dots," Burt stated as he took back the gun. I decided to give Burt a little extra room and backed away about twenty feet. Burt just grinned at me, took aim and fired. This can exploded as well.

"Just a bit more kick is all," commented Burt as he admired his shot.

"I can't wait any longer. I'm gonna try a Super Shell," he said impatiently as he loaded a three-dot into the gun.

"Here goes nothing," he said as he took aim at the furthest can.

Burt's aim must have been off as the can sat there untouched after he fired.

"Ha! You missed!" I said smugly as I turned to look at him.

What I saw took the smile right off my face. Burt was sitting on the ground – his face, streaked with black, was also decorated with several small cuts.

"You ok?" I shouted as I ran over to him.

"Yea, I'm fine. Just some nicks," he said as I helped him to his feet.

I was about to asked what happened when we both noticed the gun lying on the ground.

"My dad's gonna kill me! Look at this!" Burt said as he picked up what was once a shotgun. The barrel had a large bulge in it – like somebody had stuck a marble in a milk straw – as well as a number of small holes.

"Man, you could be blind, or even dead! That coulda blown your head off," I said rather shaken by what had just happened.

"Yea, but it didn't. And now we know just how much extra powder we can add," he said triumphantly.

"What are you gonna tell your Dad?" I asked as we began to walk home.

"I'll just tell him the gun jammed," Burt stated.

As we walked up to Burt's yard it occurred to me he was right. The gun did jam, sorta… it was jammed with too much powder.

Chapter 11

NINE TO TWO

Most boys seem to be competitive – from birth. Shoot, within an hour of meeting each other Burt and I got in a gnarly wreck in an attempt to figure out who was faster.

We turned everything into a competition. If Burt jumped his bike 20 feet, I would jump mine until I beat his mark. When I did 50 pushups in class, Burt would do 51. We even made eating competitive; you name it, tacos, hamburgers, pizza, even chicken nuggets became victories to brag about.

When it came to hunting, however, our competition took on a whole 'nother level of intensity. Once we figured out how to safely reload our own shotgun shells, our number one goal every season was to see who could bag the most quail, chukar, dove, or ducks with a single shot. We only had one simple rule – no shot counted unless we were together. This would eliminate any "stretching of the truth."

One snowy October morning Burt and I decided to give our teachers a day off and stay home to hunt quail. We drove the Rambler down to the bus stop to make it look like we went to school. We just slid down in the front seat and waited till the bus pulled away. This way we could hunt until the bus returned.

Burt and I loaded up our gear and headed straight to the river. We were going to hunt one of my favorite areas: Boulder Canyon. The name came about simple enough. You see, shortly after I moved to Onyx, I gave all the mountains, valleys, and other areas a name. Boulder Canyon just happened to be full of, well... boulders.

Original, huh?

Now, quail hunting in perfect weather can be difficult enough, but in the snow it can be down right impossible. Burt and I found a nice dry spot at the base of a boulder and sat down to watch the flakes come down.

"Quail are a pain in the butt when it snows," whispered my friend.

"Yea, they tend to fly in short ziggy-zaggy flights. They seem to hear and see better and they talk a whole lot more. Don't you think so, Burt?"

"Shush. Birds coming in," he replied pointing down toward the river.

We watched in frustration as the first covey flew within range then just as suddenly rose to the air as one and flew out of sight. We sat patiently for the next 20 minutes and were rewarded with another large covey, which flew in and landed all around us. I was about to tell Burt my plan of attack, when Boom! These birds, too, exploded into the air and disappeared.

"That's it. I can't stand this anymore. Let's split up and see if we can't drive them right to each other," suggested Burt as he rose to his feet.

"Okay by me, but remember no shooting in each other's direction," I replied as I stood and faced my friend.

"I will go down and come around those four pines down there," said Burt as he pointed to the southeast. "You circle around those huge boulders over there to the northwest."

I had to admit it. Burt's plan was a good one and kept us both out of the other's line of sight. I wished him luck and began making my way towards the boulders. The snow was falling a bit heavier by now and I decided to find myself a nice warm, dry place and see if some birds would come to me.

After walking about another hundred yards or so I found just what I was looking for - a group of five small pines bunched tightly together. I crawled backwards under the lowest branches right smack in the middle of the group. I was sitting there rather proud of myself when I heard Burt fire a shot in the distance. I was about to crawl out from my hiding spot but froze.

A flock of over thirty birds flew in and landed on some boulders not more then twenty feet from where I lay hidden. I watched with pounding heart as twelve birds grouped tightly together sat on a smaller boulder directly in front of me.

Sure, a real sportsman never shoots unless the birds are in flight. But heck, I was a cold, frustrated, snot-nosed kid, so I slowly took aim and squeezed the trigger. I climbed out of my spot and walked over to where I thought I would find multiple birds.

My excitement turned to frustration as all that lay upon that rock was one lonely bird. I couldn't believe I had some how missed all the others. But, as I hopped up on that rock to retrieve my bird I broke into a grin that covered my whole face. On the ground on the far side of the rock lay eight more beautiful Mountain Quail.

Nine, holy smokes, nine birds with one shot. I picked up my birds and began walking in the direction I knew Burt should be. He suddenly materialized out of some trees about fifty yards away.

"One shot and I bagged a double. Beat that!" boasted my friend as he walked up.

I just looked at him and smiled as I pulled all nine birds out of my vest.

"Nine. Nine. Nine in one shot! Can you believe this?" I shouted at my friend. Burt didn't say a single word for the first part of the hike home.

When he finally spoke it was to say, "Okay, nine quail in one shot is pretty darn good but not as good as seven ducks in one shot."

Leave it to Burt to rain on my victory parade.

"But I still can't believe you got them in flight," puzzled Burt as we walked home.

Maybe some time in the future, I might've told him the truth. But today I had to teach him a lesson. Rain on my victory parade, will ya?

Chapter 12

CANYON FLIGHT

Growing up, Burt and I were involved in some funny, and at times, downright hilarious situations. However, we did experience some "lucky to be alive/do not try this at home" moments. A lot of those moments included motorcycles. We were absolutely crazy about motorcycles. For us, it was all about how fast we could go, how high and how far we could jump.

I think Burt's dad knew. I think that's why he bought us both a first-aid book and med kit. Burt was always asking his dad to bring up two Yamaha 400s for us to ride instead of our Honda 90 Scramblers and 175s – he never did.

We were huge fans of Evel Knievel – the most famous daredevil of all time. When he would attempt to jump thirteen cars, we would attempt that many bales of hay. We would "borrow" them from local ranchers. Those that didn't explode when we landed on them were always promptly returned.

Burt and I did draw the line when it came to canyons and ravines after watching Evel attempt to jump the Snake River in Idaho in 1974. But we did jump the South Fork of the Kern River, several irrigation ditches, Highway 178 (over unsuspecting traffic), the duck pond in Onyx, most barbed wire fences and Burt's Rambler.

I want to explain about a jump we didn't make.

We loved to explore new areas. One such area was back behind Onyx. I believe its real name was Scodie Canyon but Burt and I just called it "The Little Grand Canyon." From a distance, you could tell it had a few steep and deep ravines, as well as (thankfully) very few trees (Burt and I had a rather painful experience with a rugged old pine one snowy morning up on Walker Pass the year before).

"How many miles you figure 'til we get up there?" I asked Burt one Saturday morning.

"From right here, I would say at least five or six miles," replied Burt. We finished loading up our backpacks with all the important essentials.

"I got four double bologna and cheese, a large bag of Cheetos, two apples plus my frozen canteen," I said rather proudly.

Always trying to outdo me, Burt replied, "I had my mom make four fried egg and bacon sandwiches, a dozen homemade chocolate chip cookies, two oranges and some water. Hey, I'm hungry now!"

Burt tossed me an enormous egg sandwich. As we sat there and ate, we realized we might as well take our guns and do a little deer hunting.

"Wow, this is going to be a pretty good adventure. I hope we at least see some deer," I said.

"Let's just hope nothing goes wrong," added Burt.

We finished our snack, loaded up our bikes, and headed out. Normally, Burt and I race everywhere we go, but that day we were content to roll slowly side by side, one hand on the throttle and the other resting on a leg. When we reached the local rancher's fence, we rode along it until we came to a pretty good-sized ditch. We simply laid our bikes on their side and drug them under the bottom wire.

"Shoot. That was easy. Hope the rest of the day goes that well," grumbled Burt.

"Shut up. You and your whining are going to jinx us. Just keep that kind of stuff to yourself," I shot back rather heatedly.

The ride up to the top of the ridge took us awhile as we constantly had to switch back and forth across the mountain so the climb wasn't too steep. Once we reached the top, Burt and I were shocked to see a nice little mesa. The entire space was covered in sagebrush with the occasional work-shed-sized or travel-trailer-sized boulder.

"Well, since we have not seen a single deer, what do you say we play tag?" asked Burt.

Our version of tag was simple. I chased Burt on his bike until I was able to slap his back. Then he had to chase me and on the game went. The only rule was you could not go over twenty-five miles per hour. We both broke that rule all the time, but we still had it in place.

Splat! Burt promptly slapped me on the back and took off. I realized I was going to have to cheat a little on that speed rule to catch him but just as I was about to hit the gas, Burt stood up on the seat of his motorcycle, launched himself off to the right landing in the middle of a giant sage bush.

Confused, I slammed on my brakes and laid my bike over landing unharmed in the soft dirt.

As soon as I slid to a stop, I jumped up. Burt was about twenty yards ahead of me just standing there with his back to me. I could tell he was upset by the way he stood with his arms folded across his chest.

"Why did you leap off your bike like that?" I asked as I jogged up.

Burt didn't say a word. He just grabbed me, stopping my forward momentum, and pointed out in front of us.

There in the center of the mesa was an extremely large and incredibly deep gorge. We were standing on the edge of a cliff with what looked to be at least a three to four hundred foot drop off. Burt's bike was a small silver and red square at the bottom.

"What... How are we going to get your bike?" I asked.

"We can get my Dad's construction wheelbarrow and bring it up that creek bed," Burt said with a sigh.

"What about your gun?" I asked.

"It's over in the bushes. Come on. We got to go, so we can get this done before dark," sighed Burt.

We jumped on my bike and rode back to the house. We drove the Rambler to the fence and started hiking in with the wheelbarrow. On the way, we talked soberly about the fact that we both could have gone off that cliff.

"From now on, we don't play tag until we know the area. I was about to cheat and add some speed," I said philosophically.

"I just gunned it and I was going to turn and look at you but I didn't. Man, if I had…" Burt's voice trailed off.

We both went silent as we realized just how blessed we were.

"There's your bike over there," I said as we rounded a turn.

The bike was scattered all over. The front forks had snapped off along with the front tire, which was completely destroyed. All the spokes were shattered and the rim was crushed. The gas tank and seat were ripped off, along with the muffler and rear wheel. The bike must have hit a few rocks on the way down as the frame itself was bent almost in two.

"This isn't that bad. I can salvage a lot of this," Burt said wishfully.

We loaded up the wheelbarrow and made it back to the Rambler at dusk.

"Look at it this way, Burt. Old Evel Knievel didn't make his jump either."

"Yeah, but he gets paid to tear up his stuff," Burt said dejectedly.

"I wonder if we could get kids to pay to watch us jump stuff. Wouldn't that be cool?" I said wishfully.

Burt just turned and smiled.

Chapter 13

ADVENTUROUS OR STUPID?

Today most young boys want cell phones, iPods, or whatever high-tech gadget currently has everyone's attention. In the mid to late 60s and 70's, however, the coolest thing to own was a Stingray bike complete with banana seat. And you better believe Burt and I were cool.

We both had the exact same bike and we rode those puppies wherever we wanted to go. Sure, we eventually moved on to motorcycles, but for a few years our Stingrays were our most prized possessions. Our favorite thing to do with them was to jump over things. We were always building some sorta ramp: ramps to jump fences, ramps to jump irrigation ditches, ramps to jump bushes, ramps to jump picnic tables. We even built ramps to jump into the river.

Looking back through the eyes of maturity and experience, I now realize that Evel Knievel was perhaps not the best role model for a pre-teen boy and "Stupid" might be a more accurate description of some of the stunts we pulled. Like the one summer's morn we learned that the-Higher-and-Longer-the-Jump-the-Better wasn't necessarily true.

Luckily, the roads in Onyx were all dirt and sand, which made ramp construction much easier. Burt and I were in the process of building a ramp in front of his trailer when another friend of ours, Billy, rode up. Billy lived in Downey and spent a few weeks visiting his grandparents in Onyx every summer.

Billy thought out loud, "You know, if you turn those bales of hay lengthwise and stack them, I bet if we timed it right all three of us could be in the air at the same time."

Burt and I smiled at each other and began to rebuild our ramp. That was one reason we liked Billy. He was as adventurous as us. Once we had the ramp completed we each took several practice jumps.

"You two take a few jumps back to back so I can figure out the timing," ordered Burt. Billy and I took the prescribed jumps.

Burt said, "Looks like we need to be about five seconds apart – that way one will be coming down, one will be at the top, and one will be on the way up. This is gonna be so cool."

We picked the order the way we always did with two rounds of Rock-Paper-Scissors. I tried to not smile too large when I won the top spot. The order would be: Burt, me, then Billy.

"I'm gonna get my mom to come out and take some pictures," Burt said as he headed to his trailer.

Burt's mom told us to each take a jump so she could get an individual picture of each of us as well as the group shot.

"Okay, boys, let's get this show in the air!" exclaimed Burt excitedly.

We all got in position Burt turned and said, "Remember, five seconds!"

Burt took off and I began my count down. I took off peddling as fast as I could. I saw Burt hit the top of the ramp and pop up and out of my view. As I hit the top of the ramp and became airborne, Burt suddenly reappeared in front of me on his descent.

Just as I hit the apex of the jump I heard Burt yell, "Now, Mom, now!"

It was at that moment when I realized that five seconds of separation between us was way too short - that, and maybe we should've had three different ramps with three different landing zones.

I've heard someone say that during a car accident time seems to go into slow motion and that all sound disappears. NOT TRUE. I could hear my screams loud and clear as I came crashing down right on top of Burt. Almost instantly my world went dark and I missed Billy screaming "Nooooo!" as he landed on top of both of us.

The darkness gradually gave way to a face and a voice yelling, "You all right buddy?"

What I remember next was pain. Pure. Intense. Fire hot. Pain.

We began to stir, trying to help each other up. When I reached for Burt, he slapped my hand away and moaned, "Don't touch me."

That's when I heard Burt's mom. She was using a few choice words that I'm not gonna share right now. The gist of it was she wanted us inside so she could clean us up.

First, we picked up our bikes to assess the damage. Aside from some bent handlebars and a couple blown tires they looked okay. We, however, looked like a bloody mess.

Burt's mom had each of us sit on the kitchen table.

"Shirts and pants off, " she commanded.

I was about to tell her there was no way I was gonna sit there in my underwear, but when I saw the look on her face I quietly added my clothes to the pile.

Billy, who landed on top, seemed to have escaped with less damage then Burt and me. He had a split lip, a huge knot over his left eye, and several pretty good scrapes on both of his legs and along his right arm. Burt's mom scrubbed him with hot water and bandaged him up.

"You keep ice on that eye, but your gonna have a pretty good black eye come tomorrow."

She pointed for me to sit next. I had a bloody little tear in my left ear that had made me look worse than I was. She put a butterfly bandage on the ear the cleaned some nasty cuts on my left leg. My worst injury was a long scrape along my back. She cleaned all the sand and gravel out and put some kind of ointment on it and covered it with a big square bandage.

"You come back tomorrow around noon and we will change the

bandage out," she said.

Burt was next but the moment she grabbed his side to turn him, old Burt screamed like a mountain lion.

"Go get in the car. We are going to the hospital. Again."

Billy and I waved at Burt as they drove away.

"See you tomorrow," I said as I turned for home.

I kept watching for their car to pull in that evening but when it got dark, I just went to bed. The next morning I was so sore and stiff I didn't want to move, but, shoot, Burt was my best friend and I wanted to check on him.

Billy was already there when I came hobbling into the living room. Billy had a huge black eye and a noticeable fat lip. Burt, old Burt looked like a mummy.

"What's all wrong with you?" I asked.

"Two cracked ribs, seven stitches behind my right ear, some pretty nasty cuts on my back, and a slight concussion. Other than that I'm fine," he answered.

"Fine, my foot! You're a pain in the butt that's what you are. Now, I'm going to the pharmacy to get your prescriptions and you all three better not leave this house!" Burt's mom looked at us daring us to move.

After she left I suddenly remembered the pictures and the camera.

"Hey, is your mom gonna drop off the film while she's in town?" I asked excitedly.

"Yea. Those pictures are gonna be so cool. Hope she asks for three copies of each," said Billy excitedly.

Burt started shaking his head and making some sorta painful sounding noise. I couldn't tell if he was laughing or crying or both.

"What's the matter with you?" I asked.

Burt looked at me - then at Billy. Then he just hung his head and looked at the floor.

"She checked the camera this morning. She forgot to put any film in. There's no proof we actually made the jump," he said dejectedly.

There was proof all right. All you had to do was look at us.

Chapter 14

CRAPPIE HEAVEN

Burt always claimed he was the better fisherman. He wasn't. He thought he was the better hunter. He wasn't. He boasted he was the better motorcycle rider. Okay, I will give him that one, but just barely. My superior fishing skills were made an established fact, however, one memorable school day in May.

Burt and I had come up with a sure-fire way to get out of school any time we wanted when the hunting or fishing got hot. We'd simply arrange to get kicked out for the day. One of us would drive to school (usually Burt in the Rambler) while the other culprit would ride the bus. All our gear was stashed in the Rambler, just waiting for us.

Once we arrived at school, Burt and I would get into a loud (and rather physical) fistfight. We tried to avoid punching each other in the face but the occasional fat lip or bloody nose did happen. Of course, we would then be taken to the office and suspended for the day. Whoever drove that day would apologize and act all ashamed then offer to give the other a ride home. (This plan worked flawlessly until our senior year. See Chapter 35 – Skipping School).

That morning's "fake fight" was one of our more real ones. As we drove away from school, we were both sporting split lips, but I could hardly see out of my swollen eye.

"Burt," I mumbled, "What was that elbow to my eye for anyways?"

"That was an accident. You turned your head at the wrong time," he replied. I might have believed him if he hadn't looked out the window and laughed.

"Where to first?" I asked conveniently changing the subject.

"I hear Rabbit Island has been Crappie Heaven these past few days," answered Burt.

Now, Rabbit Island was just a little hill that sat straight across the lake from Mountain Mesa. We gave it that name because every year when the lake was full, rabbits would be trapped there until the water went down. In fact, Burt and I had some pretty good hunting days on that little island.

"Did you hear what the fish are biting on?" I asked as we turned off the highway.

"Yep. Either pink or yellow Mini Jigs or meal worms," he answered.

"Would you look at that?!" I said pointing through the windshield.

"It's a Thursday and there are people all over our spot," grumbled Burt as we climbed out of the car. He wasn't kidding. It looked like at least twenty or so people were spread out all up and down our "private" fishing hole.

"You know, we could just wade out there to the island and have the whole thing to ourselves," I said with a sly grin.

Burt's face lit up with the idea of having the whole island to fish and explore.

"What if it gets too deep?" asked Burt.

"Let's just strip down to our shorts. We can take our poles, stringers and fishing bags. Come on!" I said. We took off our shoes, socks and shirts and placed them all in the car. We decided to fish our way to the island.

"You use a Mini Jig and I'll use meal worms. That way we can find out what they are hitting on," I ordered Burt.

On both our first casts we each pulled in a nice crappie. In fact, for the next few minutes we both pulled in fish after fish. Just like that, however, the fish stopped biting. We were still about a hundred yards from the island and the water was only up to our waists.

"Let's get to the island. We can fish this area on the way back," Burt suggested.

"Fine by me. I can't wait to get on the island anyway." I answered back.

We walked only about another ten feet when Burt, who was a few feet ahead of me, suddenly disappeared. His pole, then his head popped back out of the water.

"It drops off really quick here," he said dryly. "Let me dog-paddle my way forward and see if I can stand up."

I watched him energetically splash his way forward. After he had covered another twenty to thirty feet, Burt turned around to look at me. Looking for an easier route, I had moved about fifty feet to our right and was walking calmly towards the island in only thigh deep water.

"Just shut up. Don't say a thing!" said Burt as he worked his way toward me.

I knew I needed to get back in his good graces so I reached into my fishing bag (that old pillow case cut in half and tied together with string) and pulled out a watertight bag of bologna and cheese sandwiches.

"Here. Have one of these buddy," I smiled. After polishing off two sandwiches each Burt was in a much better mood. We began to fish our way along the shore and we soon hit another hot spot. Every cast brought in a fish and in less then ten minutes we each had a full stringer.

"I bet we have at least twenty crappie each. Let's go count these puppies, " I said as I waded onto the island.

"I got eighteen crappie, two big old bluegill and a nice trout," announced Burt. "That's twenty-one. Beat that!"

"I got a total of only twenty: two trout, five bluegill and the rest are crappie," I lied.

"Okay. First person to twenty-five wins. Winner only cleans twenty. Loser has to clean thirty," challenged Burt.

"You're on," I shouted as I cast out into the lake. Now the truth is

I actually had twenty-four fish on my stringer. I knew old Burt would come up with some kind of contest.

"Twenty-two " shouted Burt as he hauled in a nice bluegill.

"Look at that, buddy. Number 25!" I hollered as I landed a monster Crappie. "I win. Old Wiggy is the Big Winner!"

"No way. You said you only had twenty!"

"I'm sorry buddy. I must of miscounted or something," I said laughing. Burt counted my fish three times.

"I can't believe you cheated and there's no way am I gonna clean thirty, " he grumbled.

"A bet's a bet," I argued.

No matter what I said Burt insisted I had cheated and we would each clean our own fish. We headed back towards the mainland with our fish in tow. The wind had come up and was making it pretty difficult to wade back to shore.

Burt, still stewing on his loss, was about twenty feet in front of me when he suddenly let out a scream and dove under water. About that time I felt something drag across my legs. Instinctively I kicked out. Imagine my surprise when Burt's complete stringer of fish wrapped around my leg.

Burt had popped up again and I asked, "Whatcha doing?"

"Oh, man. My whole stinger came loose from my belt loop. I've lost my whole stringer," Burt cried.

"I will look over this way. You keep searching over there," I said as I splashed around a bit. I watched Burt dive and disappear like a duck for the next twenty minutes.

Every time he looked my way I would splash around and holler, "Nothing yet!"

Finally, he just gave up and sloshed his way dejectedly to shore. I followed along not saying a word, just hanging my head as well. When we reached waist deep water I could contain myself no longer. I just started laughing. Burt turned around and I held up his stringer.

"How long? How long have you had them?" roared Burt.

"They swam right into me while you were doing your "Duck

Impersonations." It was just too much fun to watch."

Burt looked at me and for a moment I thought he was gonna punch my lights out but he suddenly threw his head back and started laughing.

"I guess I would have done the same thing... I bet I looked pretty funny out there."

"You did. And you know Burt, technically speaking; I caught every one of these fish. In fact, I caught twenty two at the same time."

We cleaned that mess of fish together and had one heck of a fish fry.

Chapter 15

THE DITCH

Summers in the Kern River Valley, especially in Onyx, can get pretty HOT. To escape the heat, Burt and I had several sources of cool refreshment. The first was Burt's garage: home to his pool table, a freezer, a refrigerator (always stocked with plenty of soda pop), four strategically placed fans, and a good old swamp cooler.

However, when more cooling was needed, we would dunk ourselves in water. We had the South Fork of the Kern River but our favorite swimming hole was the Onyx Ranch irrigation ditches. It was sorta like having our own water park.

Our number one spot was right alongside Highway 178 just below Onyx. This particular ditch flowed under the highway from the river and opened up to a motel-sized pool under this big, old cottonwood tree. While most of the ditches carried only about two feet of water, this hole had a deep end – about six feet – and flowed out to about two feet at the shallow end.

This was the perfect spot to cool off. We would take turns floating through the pipe under the road to pop out into our swimming hole on the other side. Burt and I, along with my little brother, David, installed a rope swing to the big cottonwood. We would run along the bank and swing out over the deep end and let go. That's where we learned to do all kinds of crazy flips, twists and turns into the water. It was also the site of some colossal belly flops.

One hot summer morning we were all down at the ditch just having a great old time messing around, jumping our bikes over the small berms alongside the ditch. Suddenly, Burt slid to a stop, hopped off his bike and walked to the edge of the swimming hole. Wondering what he was doing I hopped off my bike and walked up beside him.

"Hey, how far across do you think it is from here to the other side?" asked Burt. I looked across and thought for a moment trying to judge the distance.

"Well, from here straight across I would say maybe twenty five to thirty feet. Why?" I asked.

"I'll be right back. I need to get something from my house," answered Burt as he jumped on his bike and took off.

David and I were taking turns on the rope swing when Burt returned. He was carrying a large cloth tape measure and a shovel. He handed me the tape measure, grabbed the end of it and jumped in sloshing his way to the other side.

"Okay. Let's pull this thing tight and see just how far it is across," said Burt.

I did as he asked and hollered across to him, "Hey. I was pretty close. It says thirty two feet and four inches."

"We have both jumped further than that before. This should be no problem at all," said Burt smiling back at me.

"But that was with a ramp and a lot longer takeoff space," I countered.

"That's what the shovel is for. Come on, let's give this a try," he answered as he jumped in the ditch and made his way back over.

I directed David to stand back out of the way and told Burt he could have the first try. Burt took the shovel and built a little mound of dirt to use as a ramp. Satisfied with his work, Burt hopped on his bike and backed up about fifty feet.

"Here goes nothing!" he yelled as he took off.

We watched him as he sailed up and out over the water. I could tell he wasn't going to make it as he started to descend before he was even half way across. Burt hit the water with a wicked splash. Walls of water rose straight up vertically on both sides of him.

"That was so cool!" my brother yelled as we ran to the edge. I had to agree. That splash was incredible – way better than doing a cannon ball off of a high dive. Burt surfaced about two feet down stream from where he entered. He spit out some water and was smiling from ear to ear.

"You gotta try that. It was so much fun," he said as he and his bike sloshed their way over to the shallow end and climbed out.

"I went too high to clear the whole ditch but this is great. Just aim for the middle, buddy, and you will love it!" Burt said as he shook himself like a dog.

I backed my bike off and took off peddling. I will admit. I was a bit scared as I popped off the bank and sailed out over the water. But I was smiling too as I crashed into the water complete with a Tarzan yell at the top of my lungs. The feeling of riding your bike into the water and having it rush all over you was amazing. As soon as I hit the surface I was talking away with excitement.

"That's the coolest feeling ever. I'm doing that again," I said as I made my way to the shallow end.

I was about to tell David he could try it when I heard his Tarzan yell. I looked up to see him sailing out over the edge, landing with a giant splash of his own. I watched with pride as he popped to the surface smiling like crazy.

For the next half hour, we took turns "water jumping" our bikes into that ditch over and over again. We each tried to out-do the other performing some cool stunt as we hit the water.

David was the first to let go of the handlebars and enter with one hand held up in victory. I mastered a reclining technique with my feet off the pedals and up on the handlebars. Burt was the first to try standing up. It produced another massive splash.

"Do you think all this water will hurt our bikes?" I asked as we were sitting on them catching our breath.

"We can take my dad's air compressor and dry the chains and sprockets, then spray them with WD40 and they will be fine," said Burt.

After a few more jumps, Burt told us to stop so he could rebuild the ramp.

"I'm gonna make it longer and a little higher so I can clear the ditch this time."

We watched Burt finish his ramp and take a couple practice sprints up to it. Deciding he needed a longer takeoff run, he peddled his bike a good fifty more yards back up the trail.

"Okay. Watch this!" he yelled as he took off, complete with his own loud Tarzan yell.

David and I watched Burt fly off the ramp at full speed. Thinking back, maybe we should have dug out some sort of landing pad on the other side.

Burt had the speed to clear the water, but not the other side of the ditch. He came down hard with a loud thud on the other bank. His front tire had cleared the edge but his back tire slammed solidly into the bank. He teetered on the edge for a second before he and his bike tumbled sideways back into the water.

David and I sprang into action, jumping off the edge and making our way over to where Burt lay on his side half in and half out of the water. He was sucking great gulps of air into his lungs and holding his ribs.

"Hey, buddy. You all right?" I asked as I knelt down beside him.

"Fine. Just got... the wind... knocked... out of me... swallowed... some... water, too, " Burt panted. "My bike...?"

David and I hauled his bike out and checked it over while Burt slowly sat up catching his breath.

"Your bike looks fine. Your back tire blew out, but your rim, the chain, and sprocket all look good. I thought they would be trashed with how hard you hit," I told him.

"I saw I wasn't going to make it so I stuck my legs out to stop me from slamming into the edge. That's what knocked my breath out," said Burt.

"Man, you could have broke both your legs. That was pretty dumb of you," I scolded him.

"Maybe, but I didn't," he smiled back at me.

Once Burt completely had his breath back, we helped him up and out of the ditch. Walking our bikes back home, we went over to Burt's to dry, oil and fix up our bikes.

"Let's take some boards and build us a real ramp down there tomorrow. And we can dig us out a softer landing pit as well," said Burt when we finished fixing his bike.

"That sounds good to me," I said as my brother and I headed for home.

As we rode our bikes into our driveway, David turned to look at me and said, "Burt's crazy."

I guess he was right, but he was my kind of crazy.

Chapter 16

SNOW-BOARD-ING

Back in the 1970's snowboarding was in its infancy. Inventors in garages across the world were working on perfecting the concept of the snowboard. Burt and I may have pre-dated some of their designs when we discovered that a six foot dog-eared cedar fence board sanded down to a smooth finish could really fly down a snow-covered mountain.

We first got the idea one snowy Saturday while moving some wood around at Burt's house. Burt's mom had asked us to relocate a pile of scrap lumber from behind the garage to inside a new work shed his dad had just built. Rather than walking the wood to the shed and stacking it neatly like normal folks would do, we began tossing the wood in the general direction of the shed.

I grabbed hold of a fence board, tossed it and then watched in amazement as it glided across the snow almost all the way to the shed. It slid something like seventy-five feet, straight and true even though I barely put any power behind it.

"Hey, Burt, did you see that sucker glide all the way to the shed?" I hollered.

"What are you talking about?" was his annoyed reply.

I grabbed another fence board from the pile.

"Watch this!" I said and let fly with just a bit more power. The board slid smoothly across the surface and banged into the shed.

Burt grabbed a fence board of his own.

"That was pretty cool, but watch this!" he shouted with a sly grin.

Burt took about five running steps, threw the fence board down and jumped on top. I watched him "surf" all the way to the shed.

Now, of course, I had to give it a try. I grabbed the last board I could find, took a few running steps and jumped on. I guess Burt had better balancing skills than me, cause I fell off after about ten feet. The board shot out from beneath me and I landed on my back with enough force to knock the wind out of me. I was lying there trying to catch my breath watching Burt doubled over with laughter.

Suddenly, he got that familiar look on his face – the one that always spelled trouble – and said, "Grab a couple of these boards and follow me. Let's sand these puppies down nice and smooth so they'll really glide."

Burt used his dad's power sander in the new work shed and in no time at all we had four boards sanded down on both sides; smooth as glass.

"Come on. Let's take two of these over to Camel Mountain and have some fun," he ordered.

We decided to test our newly sanded boards on a fairly easy downhill patch without any rocks or bushes. Climbing about fifty yards up Camel Mountain, it looked pretty good. For once, Burt chose to play it safe, and we both took our first run belly down on the board.

"On three we go together. One, two, three," said Burt without waiting for a reply. The ride was magical. We both slid smoothly and quickly down to the bottom.

"That was so cool!" I said as we came to an easy stop. We hauled the boards and ourselves back up for our next run.

"I'm gonna try standing this time," said Burt.

Remembering my first try at the shed, I still wasn't too sure about standing up so I opted to go in a squatting position. I could bail out in case I got out of control. I also decided to let Burt go first so we wouldn't hinder each other.

Burt took off. I watched him glide down the run. When he reached the bottom, he rode the board to a stop and simply stepped off. I took off and stayed in my squatting position all the way down.

Flushed with our victory, Burt suggested, "Hey, let's hike up to the top and see what the other side looks like."

The backside of Camel Mountain was a lot steeper and the snow a lot deeper. About half way down was a section that was pretty clear as far as bushes, trees and rocks were concerned.

"That wide spot over and down to our left looks great," I said as I pointed the area out to Burt.

"Looks good to me, too. The less things to run into the better," answered my friend. We began to make our way down to the run. The path down the mountain looked smooth and clear all the way down. There was an old cemetery at the bottom and we could see a rusty wire fence surrounding it.

"Just make sure you come to a stop before hitting that fence," warned Burt. I was about to tell him he could go first when he added, "Your turn to go first."

I really didn't want to go first but I couldn't let Burt know that, so I opted to go down head first sliding on my belly. I figured this would let me see what was coming and give me an easy way to bail off if needed.

"Okay. Here goes nothing!" I hollered as I shoved off.

As soon as I got going two things came to mind immediately. First, I wish I had some kind of goggles on because I could barely see. And second, I was picking up speed way too quickly. I decided after a few more seconds – and a few more miles per hour – that this was way too fast. So, I simply rolled off the board onto my left shoulder.

This is where the goggles would have come in handy, as I didn't see that small bush until I was tumbling through it. After a few more somersaults I came to a sliding stop, looking up to see that cemetery fence, that barbed-wire fence, only about ten feet in front of me.

I turned and rose to my knees to tell Burt not to come down…but he was already crouching on his board and flying down the mountain.

He was doing great! Then, suddenly, without warning, he was

airborne, wind-milling down the mountain, his arms and legs whirling like crazy. I watched helplessly as my friend hit the ground, cartwheeled a few times and tumbled to a stop a few feet away. I crawled over to him. Burt sat up shaking his head.

"You all right, buddy?" I questioned putting my hands on his shoulders.

"I think so, but my left wrist really hurts and I can't feel my fingers. I think I sprained it," was his reply.

"Come on. I think we better head for home and get your wrist looked at just to be safe," I said.

Burt tried to reach down and pick up his board. But he couldn't.

"I can't use my left hand. You will have to carry mine for me," Burt winced.

I grabbed the boards and put them on my shoulder. We decided to walk back home around the bottom of the mountain instead of hiking back up and over.

As we walked past the cemetery I told Burt, "We were really lucky. We almost ended up in there."

I saw him roll his eyes, but he quickly outdid me quipping, "Hey, that would have been a dead end."

"What happened anyhow? You were doing great and then, wham!" I asked my friend.

"I was going too fast. I was just about to bail off when the board hit something under the snow and launched me," he said.

"What about you? You took a few cartwheels yourself," asked Burt.

To be honest, I had a really tender spot on my left shoulder and all along the outside of my left thigh. I told Burt I thought I would have a couple nice bruises, but that was about it. By the time we reached Burt's trailer, his wrist was really swollen. Burt's mom was not very happy as she loaded him into the Rambler for yet another trip to the emergency room.

A few hours later, I watched the Rambler pull back in over at Burt's place so I strolled over to see how he was. When I said hello to his mom, she just stared at me for a few seconds and walked inside.

"Is your mom really mad at me?" I asked.

"Not really. She just can't figure out how come I'm always the one to get hurt and not you," answered Burt. Burt was sporting a new cast as his wrist was, in fact, broken and not sprained.

"I think our snow boarding days are over for awhile. Well, at least until that cast comes off," I stated.

"I have already been thinking about adding some straps for our feet next time. You know, so we can have more control. Let's play some one-handed pool and I will tell you all about it," Burt said with a grin.

Chapter 17

COLD

While most of our hunting adventures centered around the feathered quarry, Burt and I never missed an opportunity to deer hunt. One of our most memorable hunts took place one snowy morning up near Walker Pass. Nowadays this area is covered with houses and trailers but back in the early 1970's it was just a home for animals. Discovering this spot while quail and chukar hunting the previous year, we saw over forty deer and decided right then and there we would come back next deer season.

As we parked the Rambler, the snow began to fall pretty steady. We loaded up and began what we estimated to be the two-mile trek to the canyon. It was pretty dark at 4am but Burt had come up with a darn good solution.

"Putting these socks over our flashlights was a good idea, buddy," I said as I followed Burt.

"Yep. Gives us just enough light to see without warning everything we're coming. Still, keep them pointed down," he replied quietly over his shoulder.

Our "dimmers" as Burt called them still didn't let us see all the rocks, roots and ruts. We moved along slowly, stumbling here and there, and finally reached the big canyon.

"We'll sit right here, then split up at first light. One of us can walk the ridge up top, while the other can walk the creek at the bottom of the canyon," whispered Burt.

A trio of Rock-Paper-Scissors resulted in Burt taking the ridge and me getting the creek bottom.

As the blackness faded into gray, we noticed that the snow, still sliding down steady, was now about an inch or two deep. Funny, sitting there like that, it seemed as if you could hear the flakes falling.

"Time to get going. Don't fall in the creek!" Burt said as he began to climb up.

He was quickly swallowed up by the snow and I turned my attention to hiking along the creek. It didn't take long for me to realize that walking the creek bottom was way too much work. The heavy brush, rocks, bushes, and snow made the going tough.

I climbed up the opposite side from Burt until I came upon a deer trail that ran parallel to the creek. I would walk along for a hundred yards or so, then hunker down and use my binoculars to search for deer. And to see if I could locate Burt.

It was during one of these scouting times when I saw Him. The one who would soon become known as "Old 36." He was a big barrel chested six-by-six buck. He was about 100 yards away on the same ridgeline that Burt was.

I took my binoculars off Him and looked for Burt. Burt was nowhere to be seen, so I put my glasses back on the buck. He was just ambling along neither climbing nor descending. Suddenly his head snapped up and around behind him. He froze.

I slowly moved my binoculars in the direction he was looking and saw what had grabbed his attention. Burt had come around a large outcropping of rocks. I watched Burt look at the buck, then at me, then at the buck with slow movements. Burt began to raise his gun.

That was all "Old 36" needed; he took off like lightning, travelling downhill right between Burt and I. With the buck between us, neither one of us dared shoot fearing we'd hit each other.

I saw if I could get down across the creek, I might get a good shot at Him as he crossed the creek. I reached the creek bottom, never taking my eyes off of Him. I was so excited as I anticipated bagging the biggest buck I had ever seen. Now I was glad I had lost our Rock-Paper-Scissors game. I was going to bag a monster buck.

Looking back, I probably should have paid more attention to where I was stepping instead of looking at the buck.

One minute I was looking at my trophy buck heading towards me in a beautiful snowfall and then – WHAM! – my whole body was swallowed up by snow and the coldest water you can imagine.

I had stepped through a bush expecting firm footing only to find nothing but creek. Fortunately, the bush still contained my gun. I staggered to my feet, retrieved my gun and climbed out of the creek bottom. I took off my hunting vest and sweatshirt and was in the process of wringing the water out of my t-shirt when Burt materialized out of the snow.

"I told you not to fall in the creek," he greeted me with a laugh.

I chattered back, "We-we-we need-need to build, build a-a-a fi-fire."

"Yeah, that buck is long gone now. Let's find a place and build you a fire to dry off," he replied.

We hiked along the creek until we found a large pine tree.

"This is perfect," said Burt.

We scraped away the snow until we got to the dry pine needles and pinecones underneath. We gathered a large pile and lit it on fire.

"I'm going to go find us some dry wood. You stay and try to get warm," admonished Burt.

"Here. Take this and wrap your feet in it while your socks and shoes dry," he added, taking off his t-shirt and handing it to me.

I laid my socks, shoes, t-shirt, vest, and sweatshirt as close to the fire as I could. I also did as Burt told me and wrapped my feet in his warm shirt.

Burt returned with an armload of small sticks, pine bark, and one watermelon-sized chunk of wood.

"I found this big old chunk under a rock by the creek. We are going to have a fine fire in no time," he stated as he began to add his collection to the fire. Burt was right. In no time we had a warm fire blazing away.

We sat and talked for almost an hour as my clothes dried. Once my socks were dry, I unwrapped my feet from the t-shirt and put my socks on. My shoes, while damp, were much more comfortable.

"We are gonna call him "Old 36." Get it? Six points on each side. Six by six. Thirty Six," said Burt with a smile.

"Sorry we lost him. Which way did he go?" I asked.

"He crossed the creek somewhere around here, followed that trail you were on and headed deeper into the canyon. We'll get him next time," Burt answered.

I was just about to answer but the heat from the fire had been slowly melting the snow up in the pine tree above us. Plop! It chose right then to dump a load of snow down on top of us. Burt and I were both covered.

Laughing, he said, "Well, we better head for the car."

I shook the snow off my t-shirt, sweatshirt, and vest and put them on. "Not bad," I said. "A little damp here and there but okay. Let's get to the Rambler and its heater."

We stomped out the remains of the fire and buried the chunk in the snow.

"We'll follow the creek for a while. That will get us to the Rambler faster," said Burt leading the way.

We hiked the creek until we needed to head up and south to the car.

"It's steep," said Burt, as he headed up, "but it's the quickest way to the car."

I followed on Burt's heels, happy to be leaving the creek bottom. My thoughts were on the heater and my lunch when my daydream was shattered by Burt's loud, "NOOOO!"

I looked up just in time to see Burt's backside smash right into my face. He had lost his balance and crashed back into me. Both of us tumbling in a mass of arms and legs, gaining speed, landed with a big splash right back in the creek.

"Holy smokes, this is cold!" shrieked Burt as he staggered to his feet.

"Twice! Are you kidding me, twice!" I yelled to the sky.

We both clawed our way up and out of the creek bottom.

"Come on," I said as I began to look for wood, "Let's build us another fire."

"We can't. My matches were in my back pocket. I forgot to put them back in my waterproof container," stated Burt.

"Let's just get back to the Rambler."

The snow had stopped and blue sky was peaking out in spots as we reached the car.

"I'm glad we're here. I am starting to lose feeling in my toes," said Burt.

We both climbed in and Burt fired up the engine and cranked the heater to full blast.

I turned to ask him a question but before I could he answered it.

"Yes, I have a full tank of gas, so relax."

After about five minutes, we both decided our clothes would dry faster if we took them off and spread them on the seat, floor, and dashboard.

So, there we were sitting in our birthday suits, munching away on lunch. In fact, Burt decided he didn't want to wait for our clothes to dry. Shoot, we were only 30 minutes from home and all the dry clothes we wanted.

So we headed home naked as jaybirds, laughing the whole time and hoping we didn't get pulled over. We laughed even harder about what we would say if we did get pulled over. What kind of look would that officer have on his face?

It would have probably been just like the look on Burt's mom's face. She was outside when we pulled up and streaked past her into the garage.

Shaking her head with a laugh, "I'm not even going to ask."

Chapter 18

OOPS!

Burt and I loved every season of the year: Deer Season, Fishing Season, Dove Season, Quail Season, and, of course, Duck Season. But one memorable Duck Season almost was over before it got started.

The South Fork of the Kern River was running fairly high this particular year. Some heavy September and early October rains had pretty much filled the river to its brim. This was great – ducks seemed to be everywhere.

So, one cold, rainy morning Burt and I decided school could do without us. We would duck hunt instead. Parking the Rambler down by the Onyx Emporium, we headed over to the river. When we got there, however, we realized all the places we used to cross to the other side were all under water.

"Let's just hunt from this side until we find a way across. It's too cold to get wet today," I suggested.

Burt agreed and we headed east along the south bank. After about ten minutes, a small flock of about eight Mallards exploded off the river about twenty yards in front of us.

Burt, who was about fifteen feet in front of me, swung his gun up and to the right aiming at the lead bird. I brought my gun up and zeroed in on the last bird, a beautiful male. Our shots sounded as one and both birds tumbled from the wet, gray sky.

"Two for two. Nice shooting, buddy," I said as I walked up and slapped Burt on the back.

Burt turned around and said with a big old smile. "You know, we have never had a day where we have both been perfect. Today could be that day. Let's get our birds and keep on going up river."

Fortunately, both birds came down on dry ground. We retrieved them and continued along the riverbank. We came to a slight bend that opened up to a great view when Burt suddenly tackled me to the ground, covering my mouth with one hand.

Now lying almost on top of me, he whispered in my ear, "Don't make a sound. The river is covered with ducks."

I nodded that I understood and we silently and slowly slithered backwards into some heavy, tall grass. Burt then pointed to some small sage bushes along the bank to our left. We belly-crawled up to them and peeked out.

There were two enormous flocks of ducks floating on the water. One was slightly upriver to our right about twenty yards away, while the other was to our left and roughly twenty to twenty five yards away.

Burt put his mouth to my ear again and whispered, "I am going to slowly crawl over to the edge by that small tree. When I nod at you, we stand up and shoot. I will take that group and you can have this one."

I watched him ease into position. I slowly gathered myself to be able to jump up at his signal. Burt tucked his feet under him, looked at me and nodded his head. We popped up simultaneously and the river erupted with ducks. I drew a bead on my first bird and fired. I quickly fired again and again.

"Three for three," I yelled over at Burt as the roar of our shots faded across the river.

"I dropped all three of my birds, too," he hollered back with a loud whoop.

Two of my birds landed out of the water and I quickly retrieved both of them. The third, however, had come down in the river and was stuck against a pile of branches about forty feet out and thirty yards down river. I quickly took off all my clothes and jumped into the cold water. I was back on the bank in no time. I used my t-shirt as a towel and was in the process of putting my socks and shoes on when Burt walked up.

"Too bad you had to get wet. If you were a better shot you would have dropped all your birds on dry ground like me," Burt teased with a laugh.

"I don't care. We are still "perfect." Besides, I am dry and warming up now," I shot back with a grin.

We laid all our birds out to admire them when I noticed with envy that two of his birds were beautiful male Canvasbacks.

"Hey, you didn't tell me there were Canvasbacks," I was upset.

"I didn't see them until they came off the water, honest! Besides they were hidden by the rest of them," was Burt's dubious reply.

"Come on. When I was picking up my birds, I saw a place where we can cross. Let's go over and head back towards Onyx. It's easier walking on that side anyways," Burt stated as he headed for the crossing spot. We made it across the river and began walking back towards Onyx.

"This has been a great day. We both have four birds and we are both a perfect four for four," I said as we walked along.

"Yep. All we need now is one more bird each and our perfect day will also include a limit for each of us," Burt added.

We walked the whole way back finding an easy spot to cross over about a half mile below where we started but we never saw another bird.

"I guess we scared them all away, but this was sure a great day," Burt said as we climbed into the Rambler and headed home.

"Well, I am 'perfectly' happy," said Burt. "Get it? 'Perfectly' happy."

Burt made a beeline for the bathroom when we got back to his house. His mom was waiting for us with arms crossed. We showed her our birds but she just stared at us, hands on hips. She wasn't fazed that we had ditched school (again), but she was rather upset we had taken the car.

"I need to get into town. It's a good thing you're not any later. I have a doctor's appointment in an hour and then I am going to the store. You clean those birds and get them in the freezer. And don't go anywhere else. I need you here when I get back," she said as she drove off.

Burt and I cleaned the birds and put them in the freezer.

"Let's clean our guns and then shoot some pool," said Burt.

I had unloaded my gun at the car and it was leaning against the garage. Burt had taken his inside the trailer when he went in to use the bathroom.

"My gun's inside. I'll get it and meet you in the garage," Burt said as he headed inside. I had just picked up my gun and reached for the garage door when...Boom! I ran into the trailer to find Burt standing in his bedroom staring up at a basketball-sized hole in his ceiling.

"I didn't know it was still loaded," Burt stuttered in amazement.

We both just stood there looking at that hole. Oops.

Finally, Burt said, "Come on. My Dad has some spare roof panels from when we had to fix a water leak. Let's get this cleaned up before my mom gets home."

We found our supplies and had that panel replaced in no time. Thankfully, the blast didn't damage any wires or pipes. We fixed the damage, vacuumed the bedroom and stood admiring our handiwork.

"Do you think she will notice the panel is a bit newer?" I asked.

"I'll just tell her, if she notices, that I hit it practicing with my nunchucks. She will believe that. I have already had to replace a window. Let's shoot some pool."

We were in our eighth game when Burt's mom pulled into the driveway. We carried her groceries inside for her.

"Did you vacuum?" She asked suspiciously as she looked around the trailer.

"Yep, I, ah, we...we sorta tracked in some mud when we came in," said Burt as smooth as silk.

"Well, this is a pleasant surprise. My, what a perfect day. You boys did well hunting and cleaned my trailer for me as well. I tell you what, why don't I roast you up a couple of those ducks for dinner tomorrow?"

We both looked at her and said, "That would be great."

"Yep. Today was a 'perfect' day. We only had one bad shot all day, didn't we, buddy?" I said looking at my friend and then looking up at the ceiling and then back at my friend. Old Burt was just glaring at me shaking his head.

"I have to be going," I told Burt's mom. "Looking forward to our duck dinner!"

As I was walking away I heard his mom ask, "Burt, is that ceiling panel in your room new?"

Chapter 19

SKUNKED

One of the coolest parts of Onyx in the late 1960's and 1970's had to be what we called "The Duck Pond" – located just up the street from the Onyx Emporium at the west end of town. It wasn't very big – probably half a football field – but when we were growing up it seemed a whole lot bigger. The pond was surrounded on all sides by a dirt berm about four feet high and six foot wide. Big, old cottonwood trees dotted the west and north sides and provided us with plenty of shade... and some difficult casting.

We'd been told never to swim in the pond but we could fish it any time we wanted. So Burt, my little brother, David, and I did just that. We would haul all of our gear down by bike or motorcycle and brag about having our very own fishing hole. Our plan was always to fish ALL night but, of course, we would usually poop out around midnight and head for home.

One summer night the fishing wasn't too exciting – as in zero fish – and David decided his soft, comfy bed was more appealing than his folding lawn chair. He hopped on his bike to head home. It was only about a five-minute ride, so I wasn't worried about him.

"You be careful and be sure to be quiet entering the trailer. You don't want to wake anyone," I hollered after him.

"And watch out for skunks," I added teasingly.

"I will. And you be careful, too," he said as he rode off into the darkness. We had duck taped flashlights to our handlebars and I watched until his flashlight faded out of sight.

Skunks and their obnoxious aroma were a part of Onyx life for as long as I can remember. Over the years our dogs, our cats, our chickens, our rabbits, our cows, our horses, and even our trailer had all been sprayed numerous times. Fortunately, we had all escaped that nasty experience on a personal level.

After David left, Burt and I decided it was time to check our throw lines, setting out to see how many fish we had caught. As I said, casting was pretty tough in and around those cottonwoods. All anyone had to do was look at those low overhanging branches. They were dotted with red and white bobbers.

Burt and I thought they looked like Christmas trees covered with ornaments. "Fishmas Trees" we called them. We always waited until winter when the leaves were gone to retrieve all the bobbers we could.

We had solved the casting problem with throw lines. Burt and I each had six throw lines spaced out around the pond. After a couple of near fistfights as to which bobber belonged to whom, we solved the problem by painting Burt's with a can of yellow spray paint.

Our first check produced a total of only two fish. Poor, old Burt didn't have a single fish. I had snagged two respectable catfish, which I added to my stringer.

"Looks like I'm in the lead for now," I beamed.

"Come on, let's see what kind of snacks my mom put in my duffle bag," grumbled Burt as he stomped away.

We walked back around to where our lawn chairs and poles were. After checking our poles – they were empty – we sat down to rest and eat. We had a lantern, a small ice chest, and our duffle bag of grub so we were pretty happy.

"Peanut butter and banana sandwiches, potato chips, and Dr. Pepper make a great meal," I said as I finished draining my can.

"My mom has a couple apples and some chocolate bars in here too. Let's save them for later," Burt replied.

"Let's catch some shuteye and then we can check our lines again," I suggested.

Burt agreed and turned the lantern down. We both checked that our flashlights were working, set them down by our chairs and shut our eyes.

"Now, no monkey business waking each other up," I mumbled as my eyelids suddenly became too heavy. It seemed like I had only been asleep for a few minutes when Burt was shaking my shoulder.

"It's been two hours. Come on. Let's go haul in some fish," whispered my friend. We made our way along our lines and were mildly surprised as the fishing had gotten a whole lot better, well for me anyways.

All of Burt's lines were once again completely empty. My lines yielded four fish – all catfish. Unfortunately, two were tiny and I released them.

"Looks like I'm still in the lead. For now, at least," I said trying to cheer him up. Burt and I re-baited each line and cast them back out for the next round. Suddenly, I remembered the apples and chocolate back in Burt's duffle bag.

"Say, how bout we have some of those apples and chocolate before we rest our eyes again?" I asked my friend.

"That's exactly what I was thinking, buddy," Burt replied with a high five.

Once back at our chairs I set down and was reaching into the ice chest for a couple of sodas when the quiet of the night, along with my eardrums, was shattered by a loud and intense scream from Burt.

He scared me so bad, I jumped backwards in my chair and the ice chest, my chair, and me tumbled down the backside of the berm. When I came to a stop, I opened my mouth to ask Burt what the heck was going on but was assaulted by the pungent, overwhelming odor of skunk.

Afraid to move in case it was still around I hollered, "Is that thing still here?"

"No, I watched it take off. It went across the road," replied Burt.

I picked myself out of the dirt and climbed to the top of the berm. Burt was sitting about ten feet out in the pond.

"Where in the world did that skunk come from?" I asked.

"It was in the duffle bag. When I grabbed the bag, it just let loose. If I were you, I would get out here in the water just in case it comes back. Besides, the water and mud will help take away the smell," Burt explained.

I wasted no time in sloshing my way out to him. I noticed right away Burt had received the brunt of the spray.

"I think me falling backwards saved me from getting the worst of it. I stink but, man, you reek!" I told him.

We stripped down to our BVDs and threw our clothes towards the shore. Burt then reached down and brought up a double handful of mud from the bottom of the pond.

"Cover yourself in mud and wash with it. It's supposed to help remove the smell," he said.

"Who told you that?" I asked as I began to cover myself in mud as well.

"I read it in a hunting magazine. This guy's dogs got sprayed and that's what he did. I figure if it works for dogs, it will work for us," Burt stated.

After covering ourselves completely with mud, we then washed it off with water. I have to admit the skunk smell was almost gone. Unfortunately, it had been replaced by the mud odor, which was pretty stinky itself. We sloshed over to our cut offs and t-shirts and washed them with mud and rinsed them several times with water. My clothes were pretty much skunk free. Burt's, however, were still stinky.

"Come on, let's take our clothes and head to my house. We can wash ourselves and our clothes with laundry soap and the water hose," said Burt as we climbed out of the pond.

We left the rest of our stuff where it was and placing our wet clothes on our laps, peddled our way to Burt's. As soon as we coasted to a stop outside Burt's garage, he quietly slipped inside. He emerged moments later with two clean shirts and two pairs of shorts.

"After we wash up, we can leave our old clothes soaking in the garage sink and head back down for our stuff," said Burt.

Back at the pond, we gathered up our poles, lantern and chairs. Burt had brought along a trash bag for the duffle bag, which he was just going to throw away. We then went to pick up our throw lines. Burt's lines were empty again, while I added three more catfish to my night's work. I could tell old Burt wasn't too happy so I didn't say a thing. This time.

However, as we were walking our bikes home with all of our stuff, I couldn't help myself and began to laugh.

"What's so funny?" Burt asked just a bit annoyed.

"Well, it's just that you got 'skunked' twice tonight," I replied.

Chapter 20

THE BARN, THE BEAR,
AND THE POST

Living in the Kern River Valley, Burt and I came in contact with all kinds of wildlife. Snakes, deer, quail, coyotes, and bobcats were almost weekly encounters but one memorable fall we had a rather interesting night with a bear. Maybe.

I was feeding our chickens and harvesting their eggs one morning when Burt popped up over the fence.

"Fish and Game just drove by with a trailer trap. Let's go!" he said. We had heard talk around town that a bear had been spotted in the area. We hadn't put much stock in the rumors.

"I wonder where they're gonna put it?" I yelled from the back of Burt's motorcycle. We pulled up alongside a barbed wire fence about a mile and half from my house. The two Fish and Game guys were in the process of unhooking the trailer as Burt and I moseyed up.

"Is that a bear trap?" asked Burt.

The older of the two, a pleasant looking Santa Claus clone, replied, "Yep. It seems we have a bear around and it's been after some people's chickens and animals. You boys need to keep away from this trap."

He then proceeded to explain how the trap worked and that they would be checking it every morning.

"Do you think he might come into town?" I asked. "We've got chickens and a horse."

"You might want to keep an eye out," he said with a wink. Burt and I thanked him, promised we wouldn't bother the trap and headed home.

"Burt, I wonder if I should stand guard?" I queried as we climbed off his bike.

"I'm not gonna be on the ground with no bear," was his flat reply.

"What about the barn roof? We could sit up there. We could take our guns and flashlights."

That was pretty much the extent of our planning. I guess you could say Burt and I just went with our first thought. It was simpler that way. After dinner, I told my sisters and brother what I was gonna do.

"Maybe you should call Dad and see what he thinks?" My older sister, Sherrie, voiced her concern. Well, Dad worked and lived in Los Angeles Monday through Friday and came home on the weekends. This being a Thursday, I wasn't keen to wait that long.

"Me and Burt will be fine. You don't want anything to happen to our chickens or horse do you? Besides, Dad wouldn't mind."

Heading out the door, I yelled, "You all stay inside!"

Burt was already at the barn when I got there. I pulled a ladder out and we hauled everything up to the roof. Burt had brought his 30-30, a sleeping bag, canteen and a bag of snacks. We were ready to stay all night if need be.

Remembering last duck season when Burt's gun accidentally went off and blew a hold in his bedroom ceiling, we decided to load our guns but not chamber a round unless we had to.

Our barn had a pretty steep roof but it flattened out over the horse pen. This was perfect. We reclined back and began discussing what it would be like to fly in outer space. I don't know who fell asleep first, but Burt's elbow to my ribs brought me wide-awake.

"It's 12:45am and we have school in the morning. I'm gonna go home. No bear tonight," he stated.

We unloaded our guns and hauled everything back down the ladder.

"I'll just leave all my stuff on your porch tonight," said Burt.

"Good thinking," I said as I shone the flashlight so he could see to get over the fence. As Burt made his way across the yard, our neighbors' dogs started going nuts.

"Bear!" we both whispered simultaneously.

"I'm going to run and dive over the fence and get inside," said Burt.

I watched as he sprinted the twenty-five yards or so and leaped to fly over the fence. It was then I heard the "thud." I watched in amazement as Burt's forward progress was stopped in midair and he fell like a cinder block straight down. No sooner had he hit the ground than he was up again and clawing his way over the fence.

"What happened?" I yelled out to him.

"Fence post," was his cryptic reply.

The next morning I went out to feed the chickens. When I was finished, I grabbed Burt's gun and gear and headed over to his house. I thought it rather strange he had not come to get them already. He valued his gun above all things except maybe his motorcycle and would not leave it lying around for long on our front porch.

The Rambler was just pulling into the driveway when I got to Burt's house. Burt and his mom were in the car. At least I thought it was Burt. His head was wrapped in a bandage and his left eye was covered with a big, old patch.

My "Morning, m'am," was greeted with a long stare.

"You two..." she began and then walked into her trailer shaking her head.

"What happened to you?" I asked.

"Remember when I dove over the fence? Well, I dove straight into one of those iron fence posts. Eleven stitches and a mild concussion," he announced rather proudly.

"Come on. Let's shoot a game of pool before you head for school. I'm staying home."

"You think you can play with your eye like that?" I asked.

Burt just smiled and handed me a bandana.

"Cover up your left eye and we will be even. I'll break!

Chapter 21

RAIN

Rain. I love the sound of rain. I love the way it makes everything smell clean and new. I even enjoy being out in the rain.

"Perfect hunting weather," I observed. Usually I rode the bus to school but one rainy November morning I caught a ride with Burt in his Rambler.

"Rain isn't my favorite, but quail don't fly as much when it's wet," grumbled Burt.

We needed to stop for gas at the little store. The "little store" was what we called the Onyx Emporium – a house that had been converted to a store and post office. (Further down the road was the older Onyx Store which featured a butcher shop and carried feed and grain.)

During cold weather, the Onyx Emporium always had a fire going which made it a great place to hang out. I was pumping the gas while Burt went in to pay. I was absent-mindedly staring across the river, when suddenly a huge covey of quail rose up and took flight. I bet there were at least eighty birds winging away.

"I don't think I'll make it to school today," said a voice over my shoulder. "My throat seems to be sore."

A fake cough ensued. I turned to see Burt, grinning like a farm cat who'd just eaten two chicks, holding new boxes of shotgun shells in each hand. He'd bought more than a tank of gas.

"Well, I can't leave my best friend home alone, not with him feeling puny and all," I replied.

We parked over at my house. While I went in to change, he snuck back to his house to grab his own gear. We didn't want his mom to catch us ditching school... again. The last time she chewed him out pretty good and took away his motorcycle for a week. But what bothered me most was the whole time she was hollering at Burt, she never once looked at him. She just stared straight at me.

After loading up, we headed down to the river, parking the Rambler in a little gully that would keep it out of sight. Just before we left, Burt placed a duffle bag on the front seat and put his keys underneath the driver-side floor mat. I didn't even need to ask. The duffle bag contained a change of clothes for each of us, along with a couple towels and a pairs of old hunting boots. We had learned our lesson about the need for dry clothes as well as the importance of leaving the keys safely behind.

"Let's see if we can scare up those quail we saw," said Burt as we took off at a slight jog.

The rain was light but steady. Burt was a few feet in front of me as we rounded a bend in the path. Suddenly, birds exploded from the bushes all around us. I turned and fired three shots as fast as I could. Burt did the same. Then everything went quiet.

"I dropped all three," I said as I automatically began to reload.

"I only got two. My third shot blew a chunk out of a cottonwood tree. Let's find our birds and get after them again. I saw 'em fly and set down across the river," replied Burt.

We found all of our birds and began to look for a way to get to the other side. There was a spot, not too far upriver, where it narrowed to about a twelve to fifteen foot span. A partially uprooted young cottonwood had fallen to provide a narrow, but seemingly safe bridge.

"I'm gonna use this," said Burt.

I wasn't one hundred percent sure of this plan, so I replied, "I'm gonna check around to see if we're missing anything easier."

Funny how things happen sometimes. When I turned to look for a better way across, two things happened: the rain began to intensify and a small group of birds exploded out of the bushes immediately to the side of us. I reacted as any hunter would. I brought my gun up and fired, twice.

My happiness at dropping both birds was short-lived. Still, to this day, I don't know if it was the sound of my gun or a misstep on the slippery log, but I turned just in time to watch Burt fall butt first into the river. He disappeared from sight.

The first thing to resurface was Burt's gun followed shortly by his head and shoulders. He sloshed his way to the bank and crawled out.

Trying my darndest not to laugh, I called out, "You all right, buddy?"

"I hate the rain," was his only reply.

While Burt made his way up and out, I quickly retrieved my two birds and met him at the top of the embankment.

"We better get you back to the Rambler and those dry clothes," I said.

As we jogged back to the car in the rain, we jumped two more coveys of quail. Since Burt's gun had been completely submerged and was out of commission, he didn't even react. I thought about it, but decided not to add insult to injury and make Burt even more upset.

The twenty minutes it took to reach the Rambler went by in silence. I fired her up and turned the heaters to full blast. While I was stowing the gear in the back under a tarp, Burt climbed in and stripped out of his wet clothes. He reached for the duffel bag to pull out a towel.

In all the years I knew Burt, he very seldom cussed. So when he let loose with a "Dammit!" I was stunned.

"I grabbed the wrong duffel bag! This one's full of my mom's dirty sheets and towels!" Burt exclaimed.

When I started to speak, Burt cut me off with, "Shut up and drive me to your house!"

Watching Burt clad in nothing but his Mom's bright pink and yellow flowered towel, climb over our fence and sneak into his garage in the pouring rain was a sight I have never forgotten. When he snuck back still wearing the towel, I was confused.

"Why didn't you change there?" I queried.

"I didn't wanna get caught. We are supposed to be at school. Remember? And since neither of us have a dryer, we need to head to the Laundromat and dry our fishing clothes. I can't leave a pile of wet fishing gear in the hamper."

While waiting for his clothes to dry, I asked Burt again if he slipped on that wet tree bridge or if the sound of my gunshot made him jump and fall in.

Burt looked at me again with the same look he had on his face while sitting on the riverbank; that look that said we are done talking about this.

Then he said, "I hate the rain."

True to our friendship, we never talked about it again.

Chapter 22

SORRY, BUDDY

Unlike most friendships between boys – which will have their share of fisticuffs – Burt and I never really argued. For the most part we worked out our differences, never letting it get to the fistfight stage. Well, except once. And, man, it was a doozy. The cause of our one and only fight was a chukar.

Now for those who don't know, a chukar is, well, think of a mountain quail on steroids. These birds are extremely fast on the ground. In the air they dip, turn and dive like a fighter plane. Burt and I had always dreamed of the day we would bag our first chukar. What we didn't realize was it would also be the day our friendship almost came to an end.

After school one Thursday, Burt and I were getting a pop at the Onyx Emporium. While we sat on the porch enjoying our sodas the Witt brothers pulled up to the gas pump. When they got out wearing hunting vests, we naturally had to go over and say hi.

"How'd you do?" I asked as we walked up.

"Not bad. Take a look," replied Stuart as he dropped the tailgate.

Lying across the bed were twelve mountain quail and three huge chukars.

"Where in the world did you get those chukars?" Burt asked.

"Here, let me show you," was Stuart's reply.

We walked around to the back of the store and Stuart pointed up Scodie Canyon along the east side.

"You see that little rock-like ridge about two miles up the canyon and three quarters of the way up the mountain? That's where we found them."

"In fact, we always find them there every year," concluded Stuart.

Burt and I looked at each other and then he nodded his head – first at me and then at Stuart. I knew what he wanted me to do so I asked.

"Would you mind if Burt and I hunted there tomorrow? Neither one of us has ever shot a chukar."

Stuart smiled and told us he didn't mind at all. In fact, he gave us some advice.

"Chukars will test your patience, but it's best to go after them in the morning or the evening. One of you from above and one of you from below will make sure somebody gets a shot. That's the way we do it."

Burt and I thanked him, finished our sodas and walked home. By the time we got home, we had planned out our first ever Chukar Hunt. Our plan was to follow Stuart's advice and hunt them by coming at them from both above and below. After loading up a box of shells for each of us using Burt's shell reloader, making sure our canteens were full and our flash lights were fully charged, I asked Burt "the question."

"So, who is going to be above and who's gonna be below?"

Now, both of us knew that whoever came at them from above had a pretty good climb by flashlight up and over to the backside. We had quail-hunted that area before and knew how steep that side of the canyon was.

"Whoever it is, we have to allow that person time to get into place," answered Burt.

After a few seconds, he added: "I tell you what. To be fair, let's shoot some pool. Whoever wins two out of three gets his choice."

"Sounds fair to me. Rock-Paper-Scissors for the break," I replied.

As I returned home that night, I was extremely excited. Not only was I going chukar hunting in the morning, but also I had just beaten Burt in consecutive games of pool. I don't think he was too happy when I selected to be the one to hunt from above.

I chose above for two reasons. First, everything I had ever heard about chukars said that most of the time, when frightened, they would actually run uphill (well, I think that's what I heard). And secondly, I knew that having to sit there and wait for me to get into position would drive old Burt batty.

The next morning we left Burt's a little before 5am. It was only about two miles out to the canyon, so the drive took just a few minutes. We parked the Rambler and loaded up our shotguns.

"Okay. When I get to the top of the ridge and begin to head down, I'll flash you three times with my flashlight. Once you see the flashes, flash me back three times. Then as soon as it's light enough to hunt, I'll flash three times again and we can go after 'em," I said.

"Sounds good to me, but if either one of us runs into any chukars before we hit that rocky ridge, it's fire away. Deal?" stated Burt.

"Of course buddy. Good luck."

I gave him a high five, turned on my flashlight and began my climb. Burt turned and began his hike around the base of the mountain and around to other side. Hiking up a mountain is hard enough, but hiking up by flashlight is something all together different. Despite having to detour around thick bunches of brush that seemed to appear out of nowhere, I made pretty good time.

I reached the summit and flashed my flashlight down to where I expected Burt to be. He flashed back almost immediately and he was right about where I thought he would be. Judging by the sky over the eastern mountains behind me, we only had ten to fifteen minutes till it would begin to get light.

I had to admit – this was pretty cool. I was watching the sun slowly bring the world to life all around me. In fact, I was busy watching a pair of cottontail rabbits about twenty yards below me when the morning silence was interrupted by a shotgun blast.

I jumped up and looked down towards where Burt had been. Suddenly, running straight for me were several huge chukars. I drew a bead on the lead bird and fired. As soon as I did the bushes around me exploded with birds. I turned and fired at a bird above and to my right. I watched with satisfaction as it dropped to the ground. I went and picked it up, beaming at my first chukar. After bagging it, I hiked down to where I fired at the one on the ground. It didn't take long to find another beautiful bird. Wow, two shots and two chukars. I came out onto the rocky ridge and hollered for Burt.

"Down here. I'm on my way to you," was his reply.

It took him a few minutes to get up to me.

"Did you find my bird? I saw him drop somewhere around here," was the first thing he said.

"No, I only found my two," I replied.

The next thing out of his mouth stunned me.

"Give me my bird!" It was more of a threat than a command.

"Look. I have the two birds I shot. Yours is probably around here somewhere. We'll find it," I answered.

Burt just looked at me, walked over and started to reach into the back of my vest. I slapped his hand away and the next thing I knew, he hauls off and punches me straight in the mouth.

On instinct, I punched back. Because I was slightly uphill from Burt, I guess my punch had a little more behind it and he went tumbling head over heels down the mountain. His punch had split my lip pretty good and blood was pouring out of my mouth.

"What the heck's wrong with you?" I yelled down towards him.

"You're not taking my bird!" I heard him answer.

I will admit I was pretty upset still, so I headed down towards him with the intention of continuing our fistfight. However, when I got to him, he had this pained expression on his face.

This expression wasn't due to his enormously swollen left eye. Shoot, Burt looked like he was about to cry.

"I...um...I...I'm sorry, buddy," Burt said as he pointed to my left.

I followed his gaze to find a magnificent chukar lying on the ground just under a large sagebrush.

"See, I told you. I would never take a bird I didn't shoot," I told him.

Burt shook his head and then started to laugh.

"What's so funny?" I asked.

"I bet I looked pretty funny tumbling backwards down the mountain," he chuckled.

I tried to laugh but my fat lip hurt too much.

"Yeah. You did. And my lip looks like a bee stung me!" I mumbled.

Burt and I agreed then and there never to do that again.

We hunted the rest of the morning. We never saw another chukar but we did manage to bag twelve mountain quail between us.

The next day, we were enjoying a pop on the porch of the Emporium when Stuart Witt once again drove up.

"You boys have any luck with... What happened to you two?" he asked.

My lip was still pretty swollen and my chin area below the lip had turned a wicked purplish color. Burt's eye was swollen shut and black as an eight ball.

Without cracking a smile, I replied, "You know, those chukars are tough old birds."

Chapter 23

DRIFT TUBES

Over the years, Burt and I had more than our fair share of what you might call mishaps while hunting from the same boat. Several times these innocent mistakes put one or both of us into some mighty cold water. While fishing one summer, Burt and I saw the answer to our problems as we a watched a ski boat fly by towing some kids on an inner tube.

"That looks like fun," Burt stated as the wake from the ski boat gently rocked us.

My mind, however, saw something entirely different.

"You know how we tend to have problems shooting from the same boat?" I queried.

Burt looked at me, then back at the ski boat receding in the distance, then back at me.

Then he said, "Perfect, this way we keep our distance and have a better chance of covering a larger area."

Having used inner tubes "successfully" on Prince's Pond, we were excited to try towing each other the next duck season.

We bought a couple nice truck size tubes from Frank's. The way we figured it, for safety reasons, we needed to keep about sixty yards between boat and tube while hunting. We would still be together, but we would also be far enough away from each other that we shouldn't hurt or dunk one another. We'd already located a perfect spot to use our "drift tube" – as we called it – just up river from where the South Fork emptied into the lake.

On our first hunt of the season, Burt put us neatly into position the first time he tried. There was a large cottonwood with some nice reeds just upriver from it and some reeds just down river from it. Burt drove straight at the cottonwood and when only about twenty yards away he cut the boat down river just as fast as he could go. After about five seconds, he cut the engine and dropped the anchor.

The momentum was perfect as the tube and I swung around the tree, right into the reeds and the anchor stopped him right in the middle of the other set of reeds.

"Dude, that was awesome," I whispered. Burt replied with a thumbs-up.

We had the perfect view of birds coming down river to the lake, or off the lake to the river. We had agreed to whistle when birds were approaching from our end and it wasn't long before Burt's whistling brought my attention towards him. A flock of about sixteen birds passed over Burt and began to glide down when he fired. He had waited until most of the flock was past him to give me plenty of targets as well.

Three shots fired each. Three birds each.

To retrieve the birds, Burt tied an old life preserver to the anchor line and tied my "drift tube" line to that. Then he was free to motor around and retrieve the birds. Once he had all six, he simply drove back to the floating life preserver and tied back up again.

About thirty minutes later, another bunch of birds flew in just as before. This time Burt was two for two for a five bird limit, while I went just one for three.

"Hey," I said, "Why don't we switch places so I can be in the boat and you can try the drift tube?"

"That means you need to re-position us just like I did," replied Burt.

I didn't see a problem. I figured I would do just like Burt did and we would end up right back where we were.

I lined up the boat on the cottonwood tree and cranked the engine wide open. That was my big mistake – that, and not releasing the drift line completely. I cut the boat to the left, expecting Burt and the tube to swing right and drift into place.

Later, Burt said he was yelling like crazy but, shoot, with the wide-open engine screaming, I never heard a thing.

In fact, I didn't know anything was even wrong until I cut the engine, dropped the anchor and turned expecting to see Burt in the tube sliding smoothly into the reeds.

I was shocked to see nothing. Nothing except Burt clinging with one hand onto a cottonwood branch, one hand holding his gun high and his legs frantically treading water.

"Why did you run into the tree?" I asked.

"Just get over here and get me!" Burt yelled back.

I wasted no time in getting over to him. I just couldn't believe Burt would run into a tree like that.

Before I could talk anymore Burt said, "You were supposed to let the drift tube line go completely, then gun the boat to the left. You never let the line go, so when you gunned it you ran me straight into the tree!"

I told Burt I would do better the second time but he made me get in the front of the boat so he could drive. We retrieved his ruptured tube, hauled in our ropes and anchors and headed for the Rambler.

I offered to drive so Burt could ring out his clothes and dry off but he said, "No way am I letting you drive anything ever again!"

Chapter 24

THE GREAT TOMATO WAR

Boys love throwing things at each other: dirt clods, rocks, gourds, fruit, and of course, tomatoes. Burt and I were always trying to "splatter" each other. One day, we were out by Rocky Hill shooting our pellet guns when Billy and his cousin rode up. They had a bucket full of cherry tomatoes and wondered if we wanted to play War.

The way you won War was by splattering the other team. Once three tomatoes hit you, you were out. However, if you caught the tomato and it didn't break, that one didn't count.

Burt and I would be at War with Billy and Brian. We divided up the tomatoes and separated onto Rocky Hill. Burt and I immediately took off for the top of the hill to have the advantage of higher ground. The War was over quickly as we ambushed Billy and Brian as they moved up the hill.

"Let's have another War, but this time, let's set some rules. Each side will start on opposite sides and race to the top of Rocky Hill. Also, a head shot is fatal – no matter what, you're out," Billy pronounced.

We "borrowed" tomatoes from every garden we could. Apologies to all of you out in Onyx, but we pulled tomatoes from the entire neighborhood ending up with around 75 tomatoes each.

Even with these new rules, Burt and I knew we would win. Rocky Hill was our playground. We knew every trail, cave, and hidden spot there was on that pile of boulders. We selected the south side knowing there was a trail that went straight to the top. The only tricky spot was about three quarters of the way up, about twenty yards from the summit. There was about a ten-foot gap between boulders. The drop was close to fifty or so feet and the ground below was covered in thorn-covered bushes.

Burt and I had perfected our way over this gap the summer before. We had tied a section of rope around a boulder close to the summit and laid it across the gap. To get across you gathered the rope up, ran full speed and leaped across the gap. Once you hit with your feet, you just used the rope to walk yourself to the top. This shortcut saved around ten minutes of winding your way around the mountain.

Wearing our hunting vests, all of our ammunition (the tomatoes) was neatly stuffed in our front and back pouches. We just knew that once across we would be first to the top and be able to ambush Billy and Brian wherever and whenever we wanted to.

Why I decided to go first, I couldn't tell you. I normally let Burt go first, just in case something went wrong. I ran, I leaped, I landed fine, but as I began to use the rope to walk myself up, the rope suddenly gave way. I tumbled straight down into that gap and right into a mass of thorn bushes, landing with a thud flat on my back.

There went all the ammo/tomatoes in my back pouch.

"Hey, bud, you okay?" hollered Burt.

I couldn't answer him back just yet as I was still trying desperately to get air back into my lungs.

When Burt got no response, he came down as close as he could. He was able to see me now and repeated his earlier question.

In short little bursts I managed, "I'm... okay... wind... knocked out..."

Burt was about to reply when suddenly Billy and his cousin reached the summit from the north side. Fortunately, from that vantage point they couldn't see Burt unless they walked out onto that big boulder I'd slid off of. Burt didn't even hesitate; he just jumped.

He landed pretty hard no more than six feet from me. He threw his arms in front of his face to save himself from being ripped and torn by the thorns. I know he was hurting as I watched his eyes fill with tears. He stuffed a bandana in his mouth and began to pull thorns out of his arms and legs.

"I can't believe we beat them to the top," came a voice from above.

"Keep a look out. They will be here any time," came a cautious reply.

Burt had finished removing his collection of thorns and had managed to crawl out of the bush altogether. I had managed to sit up. He walked over, reached under my arms from behind and quickly and quietly pulled me up and out of the bush as well.

"We need to pull out all your thorns and figure a way up and out of here," whispered Burt.

Pulling my thorns out was fairly easy as the majority of mine were in my backside.

We crawled through a natural tunnel between the bases of two large boulders. To our surprise, we were now out in the open just below the summit on the north side.

Burt put his finger to his lips and motioned for me to follow him. We belly-crawled on our elbows and knees down the hill until we were around a bend and out of view from the boys. Once I was beside him, Burt laid out his plan.

"We are gonna trick them by using you as bait," he began. I was about to object as he continued.

"I'm going to crawl up around behind them. In about five minutes, you start calling for help. They will see you laying here all messed up. You need to rub a little blood from your arms on your face to really get their attention. Then, while they are both focused on helping you, I will sneak up and blast them. Game over. We win!" Burt finished with a sly grin.

"What if they ask about you?" I asked.

"Tell them I just found you and took off for home to get my first-aid kit and my motorcycle to take you home," Burt stated.

We both smiled and Burt took off. After about five minutes, I began to call for help. It didn't take too long. Soon, Billy and his cousin were by my side hanging on every word. I was giving them an Academy Award winning performance. I embellished a little telling them I'd been knocked out cold and Burt used water from his canteen to revive me. I said Burt was in pretty bad shape as well from jumping into the thorn bush to rescue me.

As they picked me up, I began congratulating them on defeating us. Brian was under one arm supporting me and Billy under the other when Burt attacked.

I guess in his excitement his aim was off as I was pelted by several tomatoes right in the face. I threw my hands up to protect my face and was trying to move backwards when I stepped in the hole. The fall and twist backwards resulted in a badly sprained right ankle.

Burt was laughing and hollering, "We gotcha. We used Cliff as bait and we gotcha."

"That was pretty low to pretend you were hurt like that," said Billy with accusation in his voice.

"Well, if it makes you feel any better, I am hurt now. I am pretty sure I sprained my ankle after Burt blasted me in the face too. Can you help me up and out of here, boys?" I asked.

Billy and his cousin just shook their heads. "You fooled us once. You're not fooling us again," said Billy as they walked away.

"Burt, get down here and help me up," I hollered. "Burt, Burt, hey, I'm really hurt now and I need some help. buddy?"

Silence.

It took me a good half an hour to hobble home… alone.

Chapter 25

RIVER CROSSING

Burt and I were actually pretty good boys. Sure, we may have fractured a law or two occasionally, but most of the time, we would have considered ourselves law-abiding citizens. Sometimes our sense of adventure, however, presented us with a temptation that was just too good to be ignored.

One of these temptations overwhelmed us while fishing the Kern River. We had learned that you could catch some nice small-mouth bass by using Rooster Tail lures. We bought a variety of colors and sizes and headed out fishing after school.

Those Rooster Tails were just the ticket. Within twenty minutes, we both had several nice small mouth bass hanging from our stringers. We traveled down river to a deep, rock-wall-lined pool.

"This looks pretty good," said Burt as he cast across the river.

I picked a spot about twenty yards below him and made a beautiful cast. My lure no sooner hit the water when, Wham! I had a real lunker on the line. The dude was a fighter so I took my time and enjoyed the battle. He finally tired and I was able to land him. I was just putting him on the stringer when Burt walked up.

"Look at this dude. I bet he goes fifteen to sixteen inches and a good two pounds," I said, holding him up for Burt to admire.

Burt smiled and pulled his stringer from behind his back. My bass's bigger brother was hanging from his stringer.

"We need to find a way across the river, as most of the good fishin' holes are along the other side," stated Burt.

We hiked down river about a half mile, but couldn't find a safe spot to cross. I was about to suggest we hike back to the Rambler and drive down the canyon apiece, when Burt – who appeared to be reading my mind – said, "No need to do that, I found our way across."

I began looking up and down the river to see this supposed way across.

"Okay, I give, is there a boat tied up somewhere?" I asked.

"Sorta. You're just not looking in the right spot," said Burt. I was about to tell him he had lost his mind when he smiled and pointed over our heads.

I followed his finger to see a small metal car suspended over the river on a large cable – the name of a California power company emblazoned on its side. Burt and I looked at each other then up at the steel ladder.

"I don't know Burt. If we get caught, we could get in a lot of trouble. I bet there's a big fine too."

"Look, there is nobody around, we will just pull ourselves across and be on our way. Come on. It beats walking all the way back."

Reluctantly, I followed him over to the ladder. We quickly climbed over the chains and locks meant to stop people from doing just what we were doing and climbed into the car.

"Hey, look at this. These will make it easier," said Burt holding up the two sets of old leatherwork gloves from the bottom of the car.

"Now, whatever you do, keep your fingers away from the pulleys above us. Here we go," smiled Burt.

We each gave a couple big pulls and our little cable car began to slide across. In fact, we were picking up speed. We were across the river now and rapidly approaching the other tower.

"We are going to have to stop ourselves," shouted Burt. "We reach up on three and hold on. One-two-three."

In my excitement, instead of grabbing the cable just behind the front pulley, I grabbed on in front of it. Just like that we came to a jarring stop. When the pulley hit my left glove, it snatched it clean off my hand. I immediately jerked both my hands straight down as the pulley ripped both gloves into a shredded mass. Those gloves no doubt saved my hands from complete dismemberment. I escaped with just a nice gash on the little finger of the left hand that looked much worse than it was.

"Man, were you lucky," said Burt. "Just look at that mess."

What was left of the gloves was packed all around the front pulley. After wrapping my finger with a strip of cloth torn from my t-shirt, we both just sat and stared at the pulley.

"Well, the good news is you still have all of your fingers. The bad news is, we are flat stuck."

Stuck, we were. There we sat some fifty or so feet up above the ground and some twenty to twenty five feet away from the tower.

"We can't jump that's for sure," said Burt, looking down at the boulders below us.

"We're just gonna have to cut ourselves free," I said dejectedly.

Burt and I took turns. One would hold us in place while the other cut away bits and pieces of the jammed gloves. We were both drenched with sweat and exhausted when Burt finally cut the last of the gloves free.

Pulling carefully and slowly with our hands well away from the pulleys, we finally reached the tower and we were able to lock the car into place with the chains and clips hanging on the tower.

"Well, that's something I will never do again," I told Burt as we headed back to the Rambler.

We both decided we were too tired to fish any more, plus my finger was hurting like crazy.

We loaded up our gear and were woofing down some peanut-butter sandwiches when a power company truck rolled up.

A nice older fella walked up. "You boys just get here?" he asked.

"Yep, we were just having a snack before trying our luck," I fibbed looking at Burt.

"That's good to know. Got a report of some guys using our cable car to cross the river. That cable car is private property. Anybody caught using it would face a $500 dollar fine and maybe some jail time. Besides, those cars are designed for one person. Two people could make it flip right off the cable. You boys be safe and good luck."

It was then I noticed Burt's stringer of fish lying on the Rambler's tailgate.

"I hear the small mouth bass are biting," he said with a grin as he headed down river toward the cable car. We watched until he disappeared around the bend.

"Next time we are going across one at a time," smiled Burt.

"There ain't gonna be no next time," I replied.

Chapter 26

CRAZY CRAPPIE

In the 1970's it seemed like Lake Isabella was always full and all varieties of fish in it were eager to bite. One summer, any time Burt and I went (be it morning, midday, or evening – it didn't matter) the bluegill and crappie fishing was flat amazing.

We were sitting on the porch at the Onyx Emporium enjoying a soda one morning when we overheard a man and his wife paying at the register. They were talking about how many crappie they'd caught from their boat around Paradise Cove.

As they exited, I asked politely, "Excuse me. I heard about your great fishing trip. Can you tell us what you were using?"

"Mealworms," came the reply.

We thanked them kindly and immediately went into the store to buy a fresh supply of mealworms. That evening we loaded up Burt's little aluminum boat in the Rambler and headed to the Lake. When we arrived at Paradise Cove, the shores were lined with people standing and sitting – every one of them fishing. It was obvious the "secret" of where to find the crappie was out.

"Look at all the people," I said as we pulled into the campground.

"Good thing we brought the boat," came Burt's reply.

"We can't forget these," I smiled handing Burt a pair of oars.

We had learned the hard way never to get in a boat anywhere without manual backup. Burt smiled back, placed the oars in the boat and walked back to the Rambler. From under an old blanket he retrieved a small cardboard box.

"Here," he said with a big, old grin as he handed me the box. "This is for you."

I was sorta leery and opened the box slowly. Knowing Burt, it could be anything, even one of his pet snakes. I broke into a huge grin myself when I found a brand new trolling motor. Now we had a backup and could stay out longer.

Before I could even ask, Burt said, "Yes, it's fully charged!"

Burt got into the boat. I walked us out to propeller depth before getting in. We headed east; well, southeast just around the bend from Paradise Cove.

"Let's fish that section of shore where nobody's fishing then work our way out to those weeds," said Burt.

We baited up and cast out. Our bobbers hit the water simultaneously and within seconds were jerked under. For the next ten minutes we hauled in crappie after crappie. Every single cast produced a fish for both of us. Then, as suddenly as it began, it stopped.

After a minute or two of no bites I said, "Well, I guess we've caught all of them in this bunch. Let's head out to those weeds and see if we can find another school of fish."

It took us a little bit longer then we expected to get out to the weeds. A trolling motor can only go so fast. The wind had come up just a little but it was enough to push us around. We tried tying ourselves to a big clump of weeds but that didn't work. Pulled the weeds straight up off the bottom.

"Let's just fish and drift along with the wind until we find something to tie ourselves to," suggested Burt.

The fishing wasn't as fast and furious as before but we were still catching some nice slabs when we saw the top of a submerged tree to tie up on. We both grabbed hold of a branch just under the surface and Burt tied us off. Time to cast out.

Wham! Just like before we started catching fish as fast as we could cast. We decided not even to bother putting them on the stringers and just tossed them into the bottom of the boat. Pretty soon we had fish flippin' and floppin' all over the place.

That's when those crazy crappies caused me to make a huge mistake. One rather large crappie flipped up and was headed over the side when I decided to lunge after him. Reacting instinctively, I failed to look behind me to see what side of the boat old Burt was on first. As luck – bad luck – would have it, Burt was leaning over hauling in a fish on the same side I lunged towards.

I realized my mistake and reached back in time to stop myself from falling in, but my grabbing the backside of the boat so suddenly caused Burt to catapult into the water.

To my horror, I also watched the brand new motor (still in its box) follow him. I wasn't about to have to pay for a new motor so I just dove right in after it. I caught that motor in both hands just below the surface. By the time I came back up for air, Burt was hanging on the side.

Did he ask about my welfare? No.

"Where's my new motor?"

"Right here under my arm," I replied dog paddling to the boat.

I tossed the motor into the boat and held it steady while Burt climbed back in. Once I climbed back in we just looked at each other. Then, we burst out laughing.

"That was so funny," I said. "You just went airborne."

"Yeah, it was the weirdest feeling to suddenly be flying through the air."

Taking a quick inventory: we discovered we still had both poles, both stringers full of fish and most of the fish were still floppin' in the bottom of the boat.

"Let's catch some more of these crazy crappies," said Burt.

Chapter 27

TARZAN SWING

Growing up in Onyx, away from the big city, Burt and I always fancied ourselves to be made in the same mold as the legendary literary heroes: Tom Sawyer, Huck Finn, Davey Crockett, Daniel Boone, and Tarzan.

We were outdoorsmen like Crockett and Boone, always fishing and hunting. We spent as much time as possible exploring our river just like Tom and Huck. When it came to swinging across things like boulders or irrigation ditches, well, we channeled our inner Tarzan.

We had discovered a couple really nice fishing holes on the South Fork of the Kern that produced a big trout or two every year. One particular spot always gave us no choice but to back track about a half mile to cross the river to fish it.

This particular hole was at a bend in the river. Our normal route took us up along the south side where a huge cottonwood tree met a fifteen-foot drop straight down to the river. The water's edge below was covered with brush, which made casting from that side impossible. In fact, you could always see several lures and bobbers hanging amongst those bushes.

The other side was flat and sandy. Standing on that side and casting into the deep channel at the base off the bushes was prime trout habitat. Burt's biggest trout, a fifteen incher (my biggest was thirteen inches) came out of that cottonwood hole.

We had fished our way up to that hole one summer day and were getting ready to back track to the crossing when Burt just sat down and began looking from that huge cottonwood tree to the other side of the river.

"Whatcha looking at?" I asked perplexed.

"You know… we could build us a rope swing from that old cottonwood that could swing us right over to the other side. It would only work from the drop off side, but we would never have to back track. Plus, we always cross back over about a mile ahead where it's shallow and walk back on the south side. We could attach a secondary rope up high and pull our swing back to the cottonwood. That way it would always be ready," stated Burt.

I sat there and thought out his idea. I didn't see anything wrong with the plan at all. Well, except for one thing.

"Sounds good buddy, but how are we gonna get the rope up and over that big, old branch?" I asked.

"Easy, we are gonna build a tree house ladder up that cottonwood, get above that branch and simple drop the rope over it," Burt smiled.

When we got back to Burt's house that afternoon, each carrying a trout from the cottonwood hole, we began getting our supplies. Burt's dad always had a pile of lumber from his construction business lying around.

We dug around and found all the two by fours we needed and cut them into sixteen two-foot sections to nail directly to the cottonwood. We tied those into two bundles of eight each along with rope straps to carry them on our backs.

Burt put a small gunnysack of nails and two hammers into the back pouch of his fishing vest. I ran home and got my fishing vest so I could carry the rope and a five-pound weight from his weight set.

"What's the weight for?" I said when I returned.

"That's for me to tie the rope to and toss it over the branch," Burt answered. Burt's dad always had spools of new rope lying around to tie down his lumber. Burt cut off about fifty feet and rolled it up and placed it in my vest.

"Better to have plenty. Let's meet here around 8am tomorrow," said Burt.

The next morning we hauled all of our supplies over to the cottonwood hole. Nailing our two by four "tree house ladder" to the tree went really smooth. After Burt nailed the final two boards in place, he was roughly thirty to thirty five feet up that tree.

Next came the tricky part – tossing that weight out over the branch far enough out there to let the rope swing freely. I tied that five-pound weight to the rope, climbed up, and handed it to Burt.

"You better climb back down in case I miss and you need to bring the rope back up to me," stated Burt.

"Try not to miss," I replied.

Burt missed.

Then he missed again and again. I must've climbed up six or seven times (I think he may have missed three or four times on purpose.) Finally, he tossed it just right as the rope looped over the branch right after it split into two smaller branches.

"Yahoo! That's right where I wanted it to be!" Burt exclaimed as he climbed down.

We quickly tied a loop knot, threaded the rope through and pulled her up tightly against the split in the branch. We both grabbed that rope and yanked backwards as hard as we could to make sure she would hold.

Burt then produced a roll of heavy twine from his vest. He climbed up the tree about half way and I pulled the big rope to him so he could tie about twenty-five feet of the twine to it. When it was secure, he tied the twine to the base of a bush near the tree.

"When we need to pull the rope back to secure it for the next time, we just have to pull it back over the river with the twine," beamed Burt.

I must admit the plan was brilliant. I hadn't even thought about getting the rope back to the tree.

"I'm gonna give 'er a test run," said Burt taking off his shirt.

"Don't you think we should put some knots in the rope for our hands and feet first?" I asked.

"We can put those in after. I want to see how far we swing out, then I will know where to put the hand knots and the foot knots."

Burt backed up about ten yards, gathered up all the extra rope on his shoulder and took off. He hit the edge and sailed out over the river perfectly.

"This is awesome. Youuuuu... " Burt's words were replaced by a guttural scream as Burt, the rope and a large section of tree limb smacked into the river with a loud splat. Burt landed squarely on his back and disappeared into the river. Seconds later he resurfaced and staggered to his feet in the knee-deep water.

"You all right, buddy?" I hollered.

"I think so. My back stings like crazy but I'm not bleeding and nothing's broken," he answered. "What happened?"

"Well... that 'sturdy-lookin' tree limb wasn't so sturdy after all. I reckon it couldn't handle the stress and just snapped off," I said looking up to where the branch used to be.

"I guess we will just have to tie our swing over the larger part of the branch, " he said.

"No way. I'm done with this. You almost broke your back."

Then it hit me. Burt and I had a habit of doing things the hard way. We tended to go with the first idea we had – which wasn't always the best idea.

Instead of crossing back and forth to fish the river, why didn't we simply fish the south side of the river all the way up, cross over where it was shallow, and then work our way down the north side. No need for a rope swing.

When I shared this epiphany with Burt, he looked at me blankly for a moment, shook his head and said, "Why didn't we think of that before I took that fall?"

Chapter 28

THE ONE THAT GOT AWAY

Anyone who has ever fished knows a time or two where everything seems to go just right. You know, that time when every place you try produces fish and those fish are monsters. There are those times, however, when everything seems to go wrong and the big one gets away. I never heard the end of it when I accidentally lost Burt's "fish of a lifetime."

It was early morning in late July and Burt and I were headed to the lake. We were taking his boat to where the North Fork of the Kern River empties into the lake. We had heard of some big trophy trout being caught there and figured we would give it a go.

Word on the street was the big fish were being caught using night crawlers and floating them down the main channel. We parked the Rambler over by the Kernville Airport and loaded everything into the boat. Due to previous mishaps, I ran through our long checklist.

Before I reached the end, Burt said impatiently, "We got everything, plus I brought along my mom's camera to take pictures of our monster fish." I was about to ask about film but before I could open my mouth, Burt added "...and yes, I have film in the camera."

We rowed out to a spot just outside of the main current and dropped the anchor. We were positioned perfectly. We could cast slightly to our right and let the current drift our bait a fair piece down into the lake.

Burt's first cast was a beauty as he dropped his night crawler dead in the middle of the current. My cast, however, fell about three feet short and missed the current. I was reeling it back in to try again when…Wham!

"Got one!" I yelled and began to pull him in. Burt set his pole down when I brought the fish close to the boat. He grabbed the net and snagged our first fish of the day.

"Nice one. I'd say about a fourteen inch rainbow," Burt said as he handed me the net.

I had just finished putting my fish on my stringer and tying it to the front of the boat when Burt yelled, "Fish!"

It was now my turn to grab the net and snag Burt's fish. It was a rainbow again but this one had to be a good fourteen to fifteen inches and was a real chunk.

"Ha! I got you on this one!" said Burt as he placed his fish on his stringer and tied it to the back of the boat. We high-fived each other and cast out again. We kept trading off catching fish and netting them for each other for a while and then it died down.

"Why don't we take a break and eat, then we can try it again. If we don't get a bite after a bit, we can move on down further into the lake," said Burt.

I was hungry so I readily agreed. While we were eating, we watched a couple boats go by. Each time we waved and they waved back.

"I bet both those guys really wanted this spot. Did you notice they never said hello?" commented Burt.

We finished lunch, grabbed our poles and baited up. Just like my first cast, this one fell short of hitting the current and I began to reel it back in hoping for the same result. No such luck. I didn't get a hit. I re-cast and hit the current.

"Fish!" I hollered as my pole bent hard to the water.

"Man, this one is a fighter!" I said as I battled the fish. I could tell by how much line he was taking out. I would seem to gain and get him close then he would take off. After about… forever…the fish finally got tired.

"Bring him in a little more and I can get him," said Burt as he leaned over the edge with the net in his hand. Just a little more reeling and Burt scooped him up and set him down into the bottom of the boat.

"Nice fish, buddy," said Burt.

It was nice. I reached down and picked him up. He had to be around fifteen inches and was a real porker. "I don't know whose is bigger…" I started to say but then hollered and pointed behind him, "Burt, your pole! It was bent in half like it would almost break in two.

"Man, if your pole hadn't been halfway under the bench, it would've flown right out of the boat," I yelled as Burt snagged his pole and began reeling. I quickly put my fatty on the stringer and grabbed the net.

"This is the biggest fish I have ever felt," Burt said.

The bend in his pole told me that was probably the case. Old Burt took his time. The battle lasted a good ten minutes or so.

"It's getting tired. I'm trying to bring it up so I can see it."

He slowly coaxed the monster to the surface.

"Catfish!" we both shouted in surprise.

Burt brought the beast – it looked to be ten to twelve pounds – right up to the boat.

"Use two hands! Don't lose him!" instructed Burt.

I reached down with two hands on the net, scooped him up, and dumped him in the bottom of the boat.

"Wow. Would you look at that!" stated Burt proudly as he carefully unhooked him. It was a huge fish. "Let me get the camera. Then you can hold him up and I'll take a picture of him."

Every fisherman knows, you gotta pick up a catfish carefully but I was so excited I just grabbed hold of the brute without thinking. I was just bringing him up when one of those sharp fins filled with venom stuck me.

Knee-jerk reaction – I hollered and let go. I watched in horror as Burt's prize hit the side of the boat and splashed back into the lake.

Burt turned away from getting the camera at the sound of the splash. The look on his face was one of absolute shock. My hand was bleeding pretty good but I stood there mouth open, not knowing what to say and not wanting to say anything.

Finally, I stuttered, "Burt, Burt, I'm, I'm so sorry, buddy. I didn't mean to drop your fish. He stuck me. I'm so, so sorry."

He just stood there looking at me then the water. Then, quietly he put the camera back in his bag, grabbed his pole and began to bait up.

"There are some bandages in the tackle box. You need to wrap that up to stop the bleeding," he said matter-of-factly.

I started to apologize again but Burt looked at me with a grin, "It was just a catfish. Now, had that been a trout, I would really be upset. Let's catch us some more fish."

I was amazed. I had lost his fish and he hadn't killed me on the spot. I thought I had escaped without any punishment. We fished for a few more hours and ended up limiting out with five nice trout each.

But that wasn't really the end of it. From then on, every time we went fishing, Burt would remind me, "Yep. Biggest fish I ever caught and you dropped him out of the boat."

Chapter 29

OLD LUCKY

Summers in Lake Isabella are usually just plain hot, but every once in a while a good, old-fashioned thunderstorm finds its way to the Kern River Valley.

One late afternoon Burt and I decided to take his little aluminum boat down to the lake. Our plan was to park at Paradise Cove and motor over towards Kissack Ranch to see if we could snag a few bass.

We got the boat in the water, loaded up all our stuff and headed out. Normally, we plodded along with an electric trolling motor but Burt had spent the better part of the past week completely cleaning and tuning his new prize: a used outboard motor.

"Shoot, with this thing we can go all over the lake. We can just use the trolling motor as a back up," beamed Burt.

"I'm still putting in oars. Just in case," I added cryptically.

Burt fired up his "new" motor on the first pull and we were off. I had to admit; flying over the water was really cool. We made it to our spot in no time at all.

"I'm gonna use a red Rooster Tail," I told Burt as I let fly with my first cast.

"I'm using a yellow one," replied Burt as he took his first cast. The words were barely out of his mouth when "Wham!" I had a fish on. After a few minutes, I brought in a nice smallmouth bass.

"Cool! One cast, one fish," I bragged as I tied my stringer to the boat and tossed my bass over the side. I was watching it tug on the stringer through its mouth when Burt hollered, "Fish!"

I cast out again as Burt pulled in a bass about the same size as mine.

"Two for two," said Burt.

Several more casts each netted no strikes. We decided to motor over towards a group of three partially submerged trees about two hundred yards away. Again, the motor fired up on the first pull and we were off, skimming over the surface of the lake once again.

"I'm gonna pull us up to the big tree in the middle and we can tie up. That way we can fish both sides," stated Burt. He timed it perfectly, gently gliding up to the tree. I tied us up and we were set.

I cast out right at the base of the tree. My Rooster Tail no sooner hit the water when "Pow!" My pole bent in half.

"I have a big dude!" I shouted as the fight began. I made sure to keep him from wrapping around the tree and after a bit brought him close enough to see him.

"Toss me the net! This guy's a pig!"

I managed to net him on the first try. He wasn't much longer than my first fish but he was a chunk – close to three pounds.

I'd just gotten him on my stringer when Burt cried, "Fish!" then "No, no, don't you do it!"

Burt's bass had wrapped itself around the submerged trunk of the tree.

"I'm not losing this guy. Hand me the net and come take my pole," ordered Burt.

"What are you gonna do?" I asked as I obeyed his commands.

"I'm gonna go get him. Just keep the tension in the line in case he unwraps himself before I get to him," said Burt.

He quickly took off his shoes, socks and shirt and dove in. I watched him swim over to the tree, take a deep breath and dive under. Suddenly the line snapped. I reeled in the line and set the pole down. Boy, was I gonna be in trouble. Burt would blame me for breaking his line as soon as he cleared the surface.

The first thing that broke the surface, however, was Burt's hand holding the net with a beautiful largemouth bass in it. His head popped up next.

"Here, take him," sputtered Burt as he kicked toward the boat. I grabbed the net and hauled it and the fish aboard. Burt hauled himself over the edge and wasted no time putting him on the stringer.

"That was pretty cool. I'm glad you had him in the net when the line snapped," I said.

Burt grinned at me. "I didn't. The line snapped and I just swung the net where I thought he would be. I got lucky. That's what I'm going to call him, Old Lucky."

That's when we noticed it was beginning to rain. In all the excitement of Burt's underwater adventure, neither one of us had paid attention to the weather. A strong breeze was pushing a massive thunderstorm right on top of us. Suddenly, lightning flashed and shortly thereafter, an accompanying boom of thunder rolled over us.

"Man, that was close," I squeaked.

"Hurry. Untie us. I will fire up the motor and we can outrun it!" shouted Burt.

I quickly untied the boat and hauled in our heavy stringers. Burt pulled the rope to start the motor.

Nothing.

He tried again.

Nothing. Nada.

He tried a third time.

Nothing. Nada. Zip.

The motor just wouldn't start. The rain was really pounding now. Another bolt of lighting lit up the whole area.

"Forget trying to outrun the storm!" shouted Burt.

"We can't just sit here in a metal boat in a lightning storm! What are we going to do?" I raged back.

"Let's tie up again, we can let the boat drift out and away from the trees, while we just climb up and sit in that big, old tree."

That's exactly what we did for the forty-five minutes it took for the storm to pass through. Looking back, climbing into that tree was not the smartest thing to do. Lightning tends to strike the tallest thing around, but hey, neither one of us paid much attention in science class, or any other class for that matter.

Thankfully, God was looking out for us – again – and the lightning never came close. We looked like a couple of purple prunes when we climbed back into the boat after the storm passed. Burt tried and tried again but that old motor just would not start.

"Fire up the trolling motor and get us to shore. We can walk to the car," I shivered.

"Can't. Battery's dead," Burt announced.

"I guess we are rowing. Good thing I put those oars in," I snapped back.

It took us a little over an hour to get to shore, go get the Rambler and get back to load up the boat.

As I examined our catch of the day, I laughed, "Maybe we should change the name of this fish from Old Lucky to Lightning!"

Chapter 30

HOOKED

It seemed like Burt and I always had to do things the hard way. After each mishap occurred, we'd look back and realize how we could have avoided trouble all together. One particular fishing faux pas, however, there was just no way we could have seen this one coming.

I don't know what we liked most, hooking into a big school of blue gill or a mess of small mouth bass. One late August found us on the river with the latter. We were fishing the first bridge just as you are leaving the town of Isabella heading west on the new Highway 178. I say new because it WAS new in 1974.

We had parked the Rambler after driving through the old Keyesville campground area. We usually didn't bother with a tackle box when fishing; carrying our gear in homemade "fanny packs" made from half a pillowcase tied to our waist. But this trip Burt decided to haul his big ol' tackle box in.

"Why did you bring your box?" I asked as we hiked down to the river.

"I want to be able to hit them with everything I got. Plus, I have a couple new plastic worms and frogs I wanna try," stated Burt.

We got to our spot and a quick game of Rock-Paper-Scissors determined that I got the top of the pool and Burt got the bottom.

"Why don't you leave your tackle box in the middle," I suggested helpfully.

He agreed and placed it on the rock ledge we fished from.

I headed up and cast in. I think it was my third cast that hooked my first bass. From then on it was pretty steady fish after fish for both of us. When we got to four fish each, I issued a challenge.

"First one to five fish wins and the loser buys the burgers."

"Deal," replied Burt, "but it's gotta be a keeper, twelve inches or better."

I guess the fish overheard us because cast after cast after cast netted us nothing. We decided to change lures. We had a rule that if one of us changed bait, so would the other. Burt decided to try one of his new plastic frogs. He handed me a plastic worm.

"Here. Tie this one on."

We headed back to our respective places at the top and bottom of the pool. Several minutes went by without a nibble. I was just about to ask Burt if we could switch lures again or maybe switch ends when he let out a big "Yee Haw!" I turned to see his pole almost bent in two.

"This is the winner right here," he bragged. "Looks like you're buying the burgers!"

Well, I couldn't lose without a fight so I began to frantically reel in and cast out as fast as I could. I was mid-cast when Burt let out a roar.

My head whipped round just in time to witness Burt, backing up to land his fish, trip and land butt first right in his tackle box.

His roar of frustration turned into a sharp intake of breath and then total silence. Not a typical reaction for Burt so I immediately put my pole down and raced to help. Grabbing the hand stretched out towards me, I hauled him to his feet.

"Take my pole. That's my fish but you'll have to land him," Burt said through clenched teeth. I must've had a confounded look on my face because Burt just slowly turned around.

Embedded in his backside were a dozen lures.

First things first.

I quickly reeled his fish in. It was a beauty – at least twenty inches and a good two and a half pounds. I put it on his stringer while Burt slowly lay down on his belly.

After assessing the situation I said, "Burt, some of these are only in your shorts. Those will be easy. But some are in you and they're gonna hurt."

"Let's get the easy ones first, so I can build my courage up, okay?" Burt hissed.

I removed eight lures stuck just to his pants. That left two Rooster Tails, a frog and a plastic worm that each still had a piece of my friend.

"Give me something to bite on so I don't scream my head off," ordered Burt. I gave him the leather sheath from his fish-cleaning knife.

"I'm gonna have to pull each one free. Whatever you do, don't move and make me jerk."

Burt didn't say anything. He didn't have to. The pain in his eyes said it all. He bit down on the leather and I went to work. The two Rooster tails were not that hard to remove. Only one of the barbs on each was embedded in his posterior.

"Two down. Only two to go."

Burt grunted.

I grabbed hold of the plastic worm hook, slowly turned it towards me and lifted it out.

Burt winced and spit out the leather case panting, "One more. One more."

The frog was definitely going to be the worst. He'd dug in in two different spots.

"Burt, trust me. I have to pull both hooks out at the same time or the ones I'm not working on will just dig in deeper."

"Okay. Just do it. But count to three so I can be ready," Burt said as he placed the leather back in his mouth.

I knew if I counted to three, Burt would just tense up making my job that much harder, so I placed my pliers on both hooks, starting counting and pulled them out clean as a whistle on two. I thought Burt would be mad but he complimented me on outsmarting him.

"Well, one thing's for sure. Those frog lures really latch on to things," I said. We started laughing. "You won fair and square, buddy. Looks like I'm buying dinner."

"Nope. I'm buying. In fact, if you keep this just between us, I'll throw in a second burger, fries and a shake," declared Burt holding out his hand. We shook on it. Burt was true to his word and paid for everything.

The waitress did ask why he wasn't sitting on his stool to eat.

Before he could reply I said, "He tripped and fell on a frog."

She gave me a funny look and walked away shaking her head. Burt and I clinked our milkshakes together and smiled.

Chapter 31

NAILED IT

Along with being hunting, fishing, and motorcycle buddies, Burt and I, well…we just did things together. We were always trying to help each other get our chores done so we would have more time to hunt, fish, and ride. I was out back pulling weeds in the garden one early morning when Burt popped up on his usual fence post.

"Hey buddy, can you come over and help me out when you're done?" Burt asked.

"You bet. I should be done in less than a half hour," was my reply. I finished pulling those weeds in record time and headed over to Burt's. I found him on the roof of their garage pulling up the shingles.

"What's up?" I said as I started to climb the ladder up to the roof.

"Remember that thunderstorm last week?"

I nodded I did.

"Well, it seems we have a small leak on this side somewhere. So my dad said to tear off everything on this side and re-roof it," stated Burt.

I looked around at the roof.

"Shoot, we can strip it, paper it and shingle it in a few hours." I said positively.

Stripping the old shingles and paper only took us about an hour. But hauling the new rolls of paper and the shingles up took us awhile.

"Man, nailing these new shingles down is gonna take us a long time," I lamented.

"Not with my dad's nail gun," beamed Burt holding it up. Burt's dad, who worked in construction, always had the latest tools and gadgets.

We soon fell into a good rhythm. I would place the shingles in their proper alignment and Burt would nail them in place.

"I'll let you use the nail gun for a bit," Burt smiled.

"Wow! Really? Shoot, thanks buddy," I beamed back.

Burt began placing the shingles and showed me where to nail them. Just like before we fell into a quick, smooth rhythm.

Soon we placed and nailed the last shingle. I placed the nail gun down and began to check the roof for any shingles we failed to nail properly.

What happened next has to go down as one of the strangest, craziest accidents ever.

Burt hollered over that he found one shingle that we'd missed a couple nails on. I walked over to the nail gun to pick it up. The moment I touched it, it went off. A nail shot out, sped across fifteen feet of roof, drove through Burt's work boot and embedded itself into the outside of his left foot.

Burt let out a sharp, short scream and collapsed.

I left the gun where it was and ran over to my buddy.

"Burt, I…it just went off…I barely touched it," I mumbled as I knelt down beside him.

"I know you didn't mean to, I watched it happen… you're gonna have to pull it out, so I can get my boot off," Burt grimaced.

I grabbed a pair of pliers from his tool belt. I didn't hesitate; I just wanted that nail out of my buddy's foot.

Burt was saying something about counting to three when I yanked it out.

"Wow, that didn't hurt at all," said Burt.

"Now I need to see how bad it is." When Burt pulled off his boot, we took one look at his blood soaked sock and realized this was worse than we thought.

Burt slowly peeled off the sock. The nail had actually gone

through the upper side of his foot and out through the bottom.

"That explains all the blood," said Burt.

"Come on, we need to get down and tell my mom. She's not gonna be happy," said Burt.

Not happy was an understatement. After an angry glare was directed our way, she put Burt into the Rambler, went inside the trailer, came out with her purse, got in and drove off.

Feeling bad, I hauled the nail gun, air-hose, and everything else off the roof. I put up the air compressor as well. It was when I was placing the nail gun on the workbench that I noticed it had a safety switch like a regular gun.

I went over to my house and sat down to wait for Burt to return. I was watering our flowerbeds when I saw the Rambler pull in over at Burt's place. I immediately walked over to check on my friend. Burt's foot was all wrapped up and he was supported by a set of crutches.

"Four stitches and a tetanus shot. I should be fine in a couple days. Just need to keep weight off of it for twenty-four hours," Burt stated.

"You know that nail gun sure has a hair trigger," I said.

"That's what has me confused. When you put the safety on, that thing won't fire," Burt replied.

"Maybe, when I grabbed it, I accidentally hit the safety is all I can think," I said, not wanting to admit I hadn't noticed the safety until later.

"Well, it happened. Let's shoot some pool. First one to win five games is the champ. I will break!" smiled Burt.

Burt really put some power into that break and four balls found the pockets.

"Wow! You really nailed that shot," I said trying not to laugh.

Burt just looked at me.

Chapter 32

CATFISH BASEBALL

Every now and then, Burt and I would go fish under the bridge that crossed the South Fork at the Onyx Ranch. We had pulled a few trout and bluegill from there and the nearby irrigation ditch.

This particular late summer afternoon, we parked the Rambler at the big turnout between the river and the ditch. After about thirty minutes of trying every lure and live bait we could think of with not even a nibble, we were ready to throw in the towel.

"Come on, let's go get a pop and go back to my house to shoot some pool," Burt called to me as he climbed up the embankment.

"You're on! There ain't any fish here anyway," I replied reeling in my line.

I was just placing my pole in the back of the Rambler when Burt suddenly grabbed my shoulder in a vice-like grip.

"Wha..." My interjection was silenced by Burt's big, old hand clamped over my mouth.

"Be quiet. Come look in the ditch," he whispered in my ear. We eased up and took a look. Swimming around, right below where the water was coming through the pipe from the river, were fourteen good-sized catfish. We slowly backed away and headed back to retrieve our gear.

"I wonder how long it took them to get here from the lake?" I asked.

"They may be from somebody's private pond. I don't care. I want catfish for dinner," stated Burt.

We both decided to put on a big, fat night crawler as bait and agreed to stay back from the edge so as not to spook the fish.

After what seemed like over fifty casts each with no luck, Burt reeled in and walked to the edge of the ditch. I did the same. So much for stealth. We both just stood there looking at those darn fish. A few minutes later one of Burt's mischievous grins slowly spread across his face.

"Come on, I have an idea," he said.

From under a tarp in the bed of the Rambler, Burt pulled out two old wooden baseball bats and a dirty burlap potato sack. Handing me a bat, Burt proceeded to lay out his plan.

"This is gonna be fun. We are gonna chase these fish all the way down the ditch to the shallow water and then just bonk them in the head."

"So... is the sack to put them in once we smack 'em?" I asked.

"Yep, but first I will swirl it around in the water to sorta drive them the way we want them to go," answered Burt.

We jumped in and began "herding" our catfish the sixty feet or so to the shallows. On our first try we managed to trap three large fish.

"Blast 'em," I hollered as I swung at a fish just to my right. My first swing produced a huge splash and a flying catfish. I grabbed the fish by the tail and placed it in the burlap sack.

"Did you see that?" I yelled turning towards my buddy.

"I told you," shouted Burt as he brought his bat down on a fish. He grabbed and tossed it in the bag. The third fish was trying to make it back to the deep pool but a quick, lunging swing resulted in another "catch."

Since we could not use the bag anymore to spook the fish Burt went and got a metal leaf rake from the Rambler. We decided to let one person wait in the shallows while the other drove the fish to him.

The rake worked even better than the burlap bag. I was able to drive seven more fish down to the shallow end. We started swinging left and right. When all the splashing subsided, we'd bagged four more fish.

"Okay, bud, it's your turn to drive them to me," I said as I took my place in the shallows. "See if you can get that big dude to come down here."

There was one rather chunky fish we both had our eye on. I think those catfish that remained, however, must have been the smarter ones. They would just reach the shallows and then would quickly dart back past Burt into the deeper pool.

Out of frustration, Burt swung the rake down onto the top of the pool. That did it! All of the remaining fish darted into the shallows.

As luck would have it, chunky boy swam right up beside me. I stepped back and swung as hard as I could. My efforts were rewarded as he floated up and lay stunned on the surface.

That was the moment when the sport of "Catfish Baseball" took an ugly turn. Some might say it was payback for our fun but un-sportsman-like fishing conduct – or for me accidently shooting Burt in the foot with a nail gun.

I took a giant step in order to grab my prize before he floated away. That step took me into deeper water, where I lost my balance and fell backwards/sideways. I was just clearing my head out of the water when my right foot exploded with pain.

I let out a scream then sucked in my breath. Burt had blasted my foot instead of a fish.

"I...I...I... was swinging at one of the big guys. I...buddy, I am so, so, so sorry."

"I don't think it is broke. See, look, I can wiggle all of my toes." I did not want to tell him that doing so hurt like crazy.

"I think you better get me home so I can put some ice on my foot as soon as possible."

Burt helped me to the Rambler, loaded everything up along with our bag of catfish and headed home. We stopped at the Onyx Emporium to buy a bag of ice. In his garage, Burt dumped the ice in a metal tub, put me in a chair and put my foot in the ice.

"I don't want to do this but I gotta let my mom check your foot," sighed Burt.

Burt's mom came in and just stared at me for a minute. She had me wiggle each toe separately. Next she had me flex my foot up and down and side to side.

"Well, I am no doctor, but it does not appear to be broke. We need to ice that thing off and on all night and check it again in the morning," she said with her hands on her hips.

"Now how did this happen exactly?" she asked. Burt and I just looked at each other then at her.

"Oh, never mind. I probably don't want to know. I just can't believe you're the one that got hurt this time," she said looking at me.

To Burt she said, "Get those fish cleaned and I will fry you up a batch."

She was actually chuckling as she left.

Since I had to keep my foot in the ice, Burt cleaned all the fish. He took them in to his mom and returned with the news she was fixing fried potatoes and fried tomatoes as well.

After chowing down on some of the best catfish I have ever eaten, Burt and I discussed our day. We both decided that prior to my foot being mistaken for a catfish, this was one of our most amazing adventures.

"I hope we get to do it again sometime," stated Burt wistfully.

"Me too. As long as I don't have to be the catfish again," I answered with a smirk.

Chapter 33

FRIED GREEN TOMATOES

In today's world, adventurous types have many opportunities to test themselves. Activities such as bungee jumping, zip lining, and paintball come to mind. However, back in the 1970s, Burt and I had to get a bit more creative.

I was out in the garden one morning with my "wrist-rocket" (basically an elongated metal sling shot) trying to knock a couple blackbirds out of our peach tree.

Just wanting to scare them off and not wanting to hurt them too much, I was using cherry tomatoes instead of my usual marbles. I was just pulling back for a shot when Burt's voice broke the morning silence.

"Bet you miss him by a mile," he predicted.

My targets both took off for the neighbor's trees. I turned to look at my friend. I still had the slingshot ready to fire, so I aimed at Burt, smiled, and let fly. My aim was dead on as the tomato exploded on impact with Burt's chest. His clean, bright white t-shirt now had a big, red, tomato stain on it.

I was laughing; I couldn't help it. The look of utter shock on Burt's face was too much. And to my surprise, Burt also broke into deep, heart-squeezing laughter.

"I'm sorry, buddy," I managed to stutter in between laughter. "I hope that didn't hurt."

Burt finally stopped laughing. "I have to admit, you shocked me when you aimed and let that tomato fly. I expected it to really hurt, but it was just a quick little sting," he said with a grin.

"This would be a lot more fun than our standard dirt clod fights," I said, looking at my friend.

"Yeah, it would. We could splatter each other from a greater distance and unlike some dirt clods, these tomatoes don't have the occasional surprise rock hidden inside," he answered.

"But we gotta keep the 'no headshots or groin shots' rules in place," I added.

Burt and I had both experienced the damage a hidden rock/headshot could cause. We also had felt the effects of an "unintentional" shot to the groin.

We decided Scodie Park would be our battlefield. Retrieving a couple of buckets from Burt's garage, we proceeded to gather our ammunition settling on fifty tomatoes each. Most came off the ground, but we did "borrow" a few tomatoes from our neighbors.

Scodie Park offered a lot of trees, a merry-go-round, a few picnic tables, a light pole, and a bathroom as places to hide and shoot from.

A game of Rock-Paper-Scissors gave me first choice of starting positions. I quickly took the picnic tables, pushing them on their side, which afforded me some fine shooting locations. Burt selected a line of pine trees about twenty yards away. To make the game interesting, we agreed we both had to move to a new location every ten minutes.

I fired a couple shots trying to get lucky and hit Burt through the trees, but did not come close. He managed to hit the picnic table a couple times but that was all.

Burt hollered, "Time!"

We both jumped up to relocate.

Burt repositioned himself behind a large shade tree and I lay down behind the merry-go-round.

That was the beginning of the end as Burt began to shoot as fast as he could. I wanted to return fire, but every time I tried to get to my knees… Wham! I would get splattered. Burt must have hit me six or seven times before I came up with a plan.

I started pushing the merry-go-round faster and faster while still lying on the ground behind it. I was waiting for two things. First, for the merry-go-round to slow to the proper speed, and second, for Burt to emerge from behind the tree to try and get to a tree barely ten yards from where I lay.

Both events happened simultaneously and fortunately for me a third development occurred as well. In his haste to get to safety, Burt dropped his bucket.

I jumped up on the merry-go-round, squatted down in the middle, and began firing. My first three shots splattered Burt all down his chest. He was returning fire, but as I was now a moving target, he wasn't splattering me back.

My next shot, however, ended the game.

Somehow, a solid green tomato had gotten into my bucket; those dudes are hard as rocks. I let it fly. Burt was kneeling down, looking at me and grinning.

My green tomato hit him just beneath the left eye. It was like a big fly swatter slapped him down. Blam. One second he was kneeling and the next he was flat on his back. I ran to him.

"Burt, I, I'm so sorry buddy. Your eye, how bad is it?" I asked.

Burt pulled his hands away. The area beneath his eye was starting to swell and the impact had broken the skin causing a little blood to trickle down off his chin.

"I never saw it coming and I ducked right into it. Why did you use a rock?" he said as he pressed his bandana to his eye.

"It wasn't a rock. It was a green tomato. I just grabbed it by accident. I feel awful, buddy," I replied

"Well that explains why I never saw it. I couldn't see it because of the trees behind you. Come on, I need to go home and put some ice on it," stated Burt.

I helped him to his feet and we walked to his house. We were sitting outside his garage when his mom pulled up in the Rambler. She had a couple bags of groceries, one in each hand as she stood staring at both our slingshots and Burt's hand pressing the ice bag to his left eye.

She walked over and said, "Let me see it."

Burt lowered the ice bag. His eye was swollen shut now with an apricot-sized knot just below it. "You were lucky. Another inch and you could have lost your eye."

Before going inside, she turned and said, "No. I don't want to know how this happened."

Burt and I just sat there not saying a word. After about twenty minutes, she stuck her head out the trailer door.

"I hope you learned your lesson. Now come on in to eat. I made your favorite, Burt... fried green tomatoes."

Chapter 34

THE LONG SWIM

One of the greatest benefits of growing up in the Kern River Valley was, and still is, the lake. Lake Isabella not only gave us miles and miles of fishing but also some of the best swimming holes a kid could ever want.

Burt and I would, often as not, fish until we got too hot. Then we'd just set our poles to the side and dive in. One May afternoon our fishing/swimming adventure turned into more than we bargained for.

We had taken the Rambler to school fully loaded with our fishing gear and Burt's two-man rubber raft with an electric trolling motor. The plan was to fish the southeastern part of the lake out by Rabbit Island. This time we waited until school ended to drive over to Rabbit Island, park, and launch the raft.

"I hope we get into a massive school of crappie," said Burt as he cast out a yellow mini jig.

My own cast soon followed.

Within seconds, it seemed we both hollered "Fish!" and reeled in our first catch of the day. Two nice crappies were now on our stringers. The next ten minutes we pulled in crappie after crappie after crappie. But just like that, the fish were suddenly gone.

"Whatcha say we go over to that set of trees and tie off. We can fish for a while and then cool off with a swim," Burt suggested.

I looked over at the trees he was talking about.

"Great idea. We can tie off along that small branch on the left.

And if we do it right the boat will stay in the shade."

We drove the boat the half-mile or so over to the trees and Burt put us perfectly in the shade and tied us up.

"I'm gonna keep the white mini jig on," I said as I let fly with my first cast. No sooner did my bait hit the water when "wham!" I had a fish. Unlike a crappie, which will fight a little and then just let you pull them in, this fish was a fighter.

"I think I have a bass," I yelled over at Burt.

"I hope we...I got a fish, too," Burt responded as his pole bent nearly to the water.

I brought my fish to the side and reached down and hauled in a nice sixteen to seventeen inch, one and a half pound smallmouth bass. I quickly put him on the stringer and watched Burt haul in a two-foot, chunky old smallmouth.

"Nice buddy, but I'm gonna catch his big brother," I stated as I cast out.

"No way man, his big, big brother is all mine," said Burt, casting out.

Well, either that fish didn't have an older brother, or they had all moved, because the next twenty minutes, we didn't even get a nibble.

"Well, I'm gonna cool off," I said as I reeled in my line.

"Good idea. Let's explore around the tree trunks to see if we can find any lures," stated Burt.

I smiled as he handed me a pair of needle-nose pliers. We clicked our pliers together and simultaneously fell backwards out of the raft. We swam over to the tree trunks.

"Bullseye! Look at this," Burt exclaimed. Just under the surface you could easily see three lures shining up at us. It took about ten minutes of work, but we soon had two Rooster Tails and a Kastmaster to add to our tackle boxes.

When we turned to head back, our joy quickly faded. Our raft was nowhere to be seen.

"It must have come untied!" I shouted to Burt.

"I'm gonna climb up the tree to see if I can find it," hollered Burt.

I held onto the lower branch and treaded water, looking up at Burt.

"I see it. It's floating about a hundred yards away towards the east," shouted Burt.

Burt dove in and I started swimming toward the direction he had indicated. Truth be told, I'm not much of a swimmer. In fact, I tend to "sink like a rock."

I don't know how long it took us or how far I had to swim. I just know I was getting pretty tired. It seemed to me the boat just kept moving further away.

"I think those stinking fish are pulling it away from us. I'm gonna turn on the jets and get my boat," Burt stated.

I watched my friend pour on a burst of speed, reach the raft, and climb aboard. He gave the motor some juice and brought the raft to me. I crawled over the edge and looked at my friend. Burt had a rather sheepish look on his face.

"What is it?" I asked as I lay there, totally exhausted.

"I made two mistakes. First, I guess my slipknot wasn't done right. But second, I left the electric motor on just a little to keep us in the shade. Sorry, buddy," said Burt.

I was too worn out from my hundred yard plus swim to even think about being upset.

"Well, just take us back to shore. I'm pooped," I said quietly.

"I would, but the battery just died. We're gonna have to row," Burt said, handing me an oar.

Chapter 35

SKIPPING SCHOOL

Looking back, I feel sorry for those principals, vice principals, and security personnel who were at the high school when Burt and I were there. It wasn't that we didn't like school. We just liked hunting and fishing a whole lot more.

To be perfectly honest, some days we just ditched for a couple periods. Say, if Burt had a test or if some paper was due in one of my classes. However, on other occasions, we had no intention of going to any classes and pretty much ditched the entire day.

I was daydreaming, looking out the door into the hall when Burt suddenly appeared. He mouthed the word "restroom" and kept walking. I immediately raised my hand to use the restroom.

"What's up, buddy?" I said as I walked into the restroom.

"Let's go fishing above Kernville. I heard they stocked it with rainbow trout this morning. I will meet you in the parking lot after this period."

I quickly ran through all my classes in my mind, concluded that there was nothing of importance I would miss and said, "See you in forty five minutes."

Everybody knew if you wanted to ditch, you waited until five to six minutes into the class, then left quickly. Usually the principal and vice principal were not in their offices at this time. They liked to walk the halls, saying hello to various classes and to catch any kids hiding in the bathrooms. Our escape went off without a hitch and we were soon on our way to Kernville.

We passed Kernville and selected a spot just above Camp Owens, a juvenile detention camp for boys, and headed for the river.

"What do you think we should use for bait?" I asked as we stared out at the water.

"I heard Rooster Tails and salmon eggs were hot last week," replied Burt.

I wasted no time and tied on my favorite Rooster Tail. This one had black, red, and orange feathers. It actually looked like a real rooster's tail. Burt also selected a Rooster Tail. He tied on a bright, solid red one.

On just my second cast, I hooked a nice, hard-fighting fish.

"Fish!" I hollered over to Burt who was just a bit ahead of me on the riverbank.

I brought a nice twelve to thirteen inch Rainbow in and quickly put him on the stringer. Burt and I usually tied our stringers to our belt loop and stood in the river or lake to fish. I did just that and cast out again.

"Fish," I yelled again as I snagged my second fish.

Burt was looking at me when his line went taut and his pole bent severely.

"Me too," was his reply.

I landed a second Rainbow around the same size as before. Burt also landed a nice Rainbow.

We moved on, fishing our way down river. After about thirty minutes, we were each down to needing one more for a limit. With our next cast we each somehow selected the exact same spot; our lures landed within a foot of each other.

"Sorry, I will...fish!" I yelled as my pole bent double.

Burt was about to say something when "Wham!" his pole snapped towards the water.

"This is cool. We will both limit out at the same time," Burt smiled back at me.

We each played our fish across the river. Burt's fish came in first, a nice fat fourteen inch Rainbow. I followed soon after with a slimmer, fourteen-incher of my own.

"Nice call, buddy. We each limited out in just over an hour," I said as we high-fived each other.

"Let's head back to the Rambler, put these babies in the ice chest, grab our lunch, and eat down by the river," suggested Burt.

We walked back to the Rambler, put our fish on ice, grabbed our grub, and we were just heading down to the river when Burt grabbed my arm and started jogging up river at an extremely fast pace. I knew something was up so I ran along the trail following Burt without saying a word.

We had run for a good quarter mile when Burt stopped and tilted his head back to catch his breath. I did the same and once I could manage it gasped, "What was that about?"

"Didn't you see him?" Burt asked.

"See who?"

"The principal. He was walking up from the river following the same path we did."

"Do you think he knows we are here?" I asked in disbelief.

"I don't know, but he wasn't carrying a fishing pole. I think he had a camera," was Burt's reply.

Before I could answer, Burt added, "Come on, let's go see what he is up to."

We jogged back towards the car and looked out through the bushes along the river. Our principal was nowhere to be seen. We waited a good twenty extra minutes.

"Looks like he is gone. Come on. Let's get to the Rambler and get home," stated Burt.

We made it to the car and drove home. All the way, we kept looking behind us for anyone following us. Once home, we cleaned the fish and started shooting some pool.

"Man, I hope he didn't get any pictures of us, cause if he did, we are dead meat. He will suspend us for sure," I said.

We played a few games but Burt never said much.

The next day at school, I was sitting in class when I got the strange sense someone was looking at me. I looked through the door to see Burt. He held up a roll of film.

After school, I asked him how he got the film. He just smiled that Burt-smile and held up a key — the key to the principal's office.

ACKNOWLEDGMENTS

I have read a lot of books in my life - most of them started or ended with dedications. Holy smokes, Batman, are these things hard to write. I know I will leave somebody out and they will get their knickers in a twist. So... I'm sorry ahead of time.

I've had many great teachers in my life and I have loved each and every one of them. However, three teachers really helped the writer - the teacher inside me - take root.

First is Winnie Henderson, who not only was my sixth and seventh grade teacher, she was also my principal and sort of adopted grandma at South Fork School in Weldon. She also had to deal with Burt and me! We lost Winnie here a while back and I'm just one of many who miss her.

The second teacher who had a tremendous effect on me was my high school English teacher, Laurel Matsukado. I struggled in English. I couldn't keep dangling participles, misplaced modifiers, alliteration, personification or past, present, future and past perfect straight. But this wonderful teacher saw my sense of humor and my mischievous attitude and encouraged me to use that in English class; to use that in my writing. It's funny. A few years after I became an English teacher, I attended a conference where she was one of the speakers. I sat in the front row and just smiled at her the whole time.

Finally, I am here today as a teacher thanks to the love and guidance of the best teacher I have ever known – my stepmom, Kathy Wiggins, long-time kindergarten teacher at South Fork School in Weldon. Kathy became my mom when I was eighteen and she always encouraged me in everything I did. I miss her every single day, but I daily try to be the type of teacher she was. I love you, Mom.

In addition to these women, the one man who has meant more to me than he'll ever know is my dad, Cliff Wiggins, Sr. Thanks for showing me how to be a great husband, father, and friend. I am so very proud to be your son.

This is also the time for me to thank my girls – the three most beautiful, loving women I know.

Katie, my youngest daughter, became a teacher like her daddy. She would often type up my stories and encourage me to keep on writing. I love you KK.

Naomi, my eldest daughter, decided at an early age that she would study English and become a beacon of God's light and love in the movie industry. She is now a producer working in Hollywood and shining for God each day. She is married to Chris who is an avid dirt bike rider and lawyer. I hope he isn't as crazy as me on that bike. Love you, Nemo.

Finally, I have to thank the greatest gift God ever gave to me, my wife, Angi. Her love and encouragement is why I am who I am. Each day when I wake up, I thank God for her and I promise Him I will love her and take care of her not only today but for every tomorrow He gives us. Angi, I love you and will always be right by your side. Thank you for believing in me, honey.

And much thanks to the Bear Valley Cub and Fence Post for first publishing these stories monthly in your newspapers. The challenge of providing a story for you every month helped me accomplish a goal of lifetime – publishing this book!

ABOUT THE AUTHOR

Clifford L. Wiggins, Jr. – aka Coach Wiggins – was born in the bustling metropolis of Los Angeles, California. At the age of ten, shortly after he lost his mom to cancer, the family moved to the Lake Isabella area. Monday through Friday his dad continued working in Los Angeles and the kids – three girls and two boys aged 6 to 12 – lived alone (and fairly unsupervised) in a trailer in Onyx, California. Granny kept a watchful eye on the kids from her home next door. A three sport athlete and student body president at Kern Valley High, Cliff headed to College of Idaho on a sports scholarship which he promptly lost – not realizing he actually had to pass classes to keep it. After a stint as a seasonal firefighter with both the Fire Department and the Forest Service, Granny gently reminded Clifford that he had promised his mom, before she died, that he would finish college. Upon receiving his AA from Bakersfield College, Cliff asked his counselor for a four-year school where there was lots of hunting and fishing. She sent him to California State University at Chico, California where he majored in Physical Education and English. He met the love of his life, Angi, working at a hardware store in Chico. To combat wedding jitters, he fished the whole day - bringing home a mess of bass that needed cleaning mere hours before the ceremony was to begin. The newlyweds moved to Tehachapi, California where Cliff took a job working for Kern Valley High's then arch-rival Tehachapi High. In addition to coaching football and baseball, he taught English to ninth graders for 36 years. In retirement, Cliff plans to walk on the beach and find as much sea glass as possible.

Stay in touch with Cliff at www.cliffwiggins.com or on Facebook.

Made in the USA
Middletown, DE
03 March 2024

50210465R00099